The book of
THE HORSE

The book of
THE HORSE

Paul Hamlyn
London • New York • Sydney • Toronto

Published by
THE HAMLYN PUBLISHING
GROUP LIMITED
LONDON • NEW YORK
SYDNEY • TORONTO
Hamlyn House, Feltham, Middlesex,
England
© Copyright 1970 The Hamlyn Publishing
Group Limited
Printed in Czechoslovakia by Svoboda,
Prague
ISBN 0 600 01766 4

Contents

*Among the earliest representations of the
horse are the magnificent paintings in the
Lascaux Caves. This photograph shows
a frieze of little horses.*

The Evolution and Domestication of the Horse

by Jane Marks

We know about the ancestors of horses from fossils which have been found in many parts of the world. They are recognizable as belonging to horse-like animals chiefly from the shape of the teeth and the bones of the leg. All fossils of horse bones come from rocks which geologists tell us belong to the Tertiary Era. This span of time, which began more than 60 million years ago, lasted until almost the present day. During it, mammals became the dominant animals, and both plants and animals evolved to their present day forms and distributions. The Tertiary Era is split into a number of geological periods, which are based on the percentage of fossils of animals similar to those of the present which are found in all the divisions of the Tertiary Era, and show us the changes which have taken place between the first horses, which were tiny forest-dwelling creatures, and the wild horses of the present day, and their domestic descendants.

The first fossil horse bones to be discovered date back nearly 60 million years, to the Eocene Period. They were so different from modern horse bones that they were not recognized as being horse-like, and were given the name *Hyracotherium*, which means 'Hyrax-beast'. It was not until many years later when more fossils, which filled in gaps in the story, had been found, that it was realized that *Hyracotherium* was a horse ancestor. It is sometimes called *Eohippus*, which means the Dawn Horse, but in spite of being a more suitable name, this is not really correct.

Hyracotherium was a small animal, smaller than the tiniest pony of today. Its height was about 2.2 hands, which is about as big as a miniature poodle dog. It was a woodland-living creature, and its teeth, which are small, tell us that it fed on the soft foliage of tropical forests, which at that time spread across much of the northern hemisphere. It had no defences against its many enemies, which also lived in the forest, except its wariness and its speed. You may be sure that its senses were quick to see, to hear, or to smell danger, and although we know from the size and shape of its brain that *Hyracotherium* could not have been a very

The skeleton of a Przewalski horse. These horses developed in north-east Asia and have interbred with many other races of horse. True-bred Przewalski horses are rare and only found in zoos.

These drawings illustrate the evolution of the horse's hoof. From left to right Miohippus, Pliohippus, Modern horse.

clever animal, its reaction must have been to run away at the least cause for alarm. If you could have seen a *Hyracotherium* running, you would have thought how unhorse-like it was, for apart from its small size and short legs, its back was curved, almost like a rabbit's back, and you would have noticed that its feet, had it stood for long enough for you to see them properly, were like a dog's paws, with four toes on the front feet and three on the hind. Underneath the toes were pads, like those of a dog, and instead of hooves, each toe carried a broad claw. *Hyracotherium* ran through its forest home more easily than a modern horse could gallop through trees, partly because of its small size, partly because its toes would spread to share its weight where the going was soft, and partly also because its eyes were well down its face, so that it could look forward and judge distances accurately when it had to leap over fallen branches or squeeze between close-growing trees.

One of the first features to change in *Hyracotherium's* descendants, in a way that foreshadowed modern horses, was in the shape of the teeth. The premolar teeth became larger and squarer, and all of the grinding teeth developed a similar shape. This meant that although the head was no bigger or heavier, feeding could be a more rapid process, and the new horse could spend more time in resting and hiding from its enemies than *Hyracotherium* had done.

As time went on, other changes occurred. The horses which could escape most easily from their enemies were those that could run the fastest. The longer an animal's legs are, generally speaking, the faster it can run, and the better its chances of survival. The bigger horses with longer legs survived, and their offspring also tended to be longer legged. One way of increasing the length of a stride is to run on the tips of the toes, and some of the horses did this. In time all of the horses ran on the very tips of their toes, and the claws became small hooves. Each foot had three toes on it, a large central toe, and two small 'outrigger' toes, which gave stability. There was a general increase in overall size, and some types of horse, which lived about 40 million years ago, grew to be as bulky as a present-day hippopotamus. However, all of the many kinds of horse of that time were forest dwellers, different in size, but essentially like *Hyracotherium* in their ways.

This changed about 30 million years ago, during the Miocene Period, when a new group of plants became abundant. These were grasses, which had evolved shortly before, and now spread rapidly across the world, covering the plains with highly nutritious food for plant-eating animals. The horses were not slow to take up the challenge of a changed environment and although some sorts of horses remained as forest-living animals until geologically very recent times, the more progressive members of the family moved out on to the plains and became no longer browsers, but grazers.

The needs of a plains-living animal, and the dangers that it faces are different from those of a forest dweller, so the horses which moved on to the grasslands were forced to change rapidly. Again, the changes chiefly concerned teeth, feet and legs. Grass is a very tough food and wears down even large square teeth such as the horses of the Miocene Period had. Some horses survived, however, as they developed teeth which continued to grow throughout the animal's life, wearing down, but not wearing out. Modern horses all have teeth of this sort; the grinding surface of the teeth changes throughout the animal's life, which is why it is possible to get a good idea of a horse's age by looking at its teeth. Long distance runners were at an advantage on the plains, where there was no hope of hiding from enemies, and the horses with the ability to travel for long distances were the ones to survive. They also became faster runners, and eventually lost the outer toes on each foot, which although gave extra stability, also meant extra weight, which could slow the animals down at a time when a desperate burst of speed might be needed to escape. All horses of the present have only one toe on each foot, and the hoof is in fact the toenail.

Another change necessary for survival in open country concerned the eyes. *Hyracotherium* and the woodland horses had eyes which pointed forward, but to a horse grazing in long grass, these could spell danger, for an enemy could stalk it without being seen. Horses whose eyes were further back, so that they could see all round them, without raising their heads, were at an advantage. Nowadays, horses have very large eyes, so far back on the side of the head, that they can see behind them quite well, but they cannot judge distances ahead of themselves as *Hyracotherium* could have done. Horses' brains have changed too, since the days of *Hyracotherium*. Not only have they got bigger, but very much more complex, so that a horse of today is a fairly intelligent animal, and is quick to learn which things are of advantage to it, and which things mean harm or danger.

The parts of the world where all of these changes took place varied, but many of them occurred in North America. The animals evolved and migrated round the Northern Hemisphere, for during the Tertiary Era there was a land bridge between Asia and America. Within the last million years, however, the horses native to America have all died out, and the surviving types of wild horse all belong to the Old World. These are the zebras of Africa, the wild asses of North Africa, the half asses of the Near East and south-western Asia, and the true horses of Europe and the plains of northern Asia. All of these species are very closely related and can be made to interbreed in captivity. The zebras are fully striped, the others may have some stripes on the legs, shoulders or back, although in true horses this can usually only be seen on dun or occasionally on grey coloured

A Przewalski horse at Hellabrunn Zoo.

A rare photograph of a Grevy zebra being used as a pack horse on Mount Kenya.

A great effort is being made to preserve the Przewalski horse by many zoos. This family group is in Munich.

Claimed to be a Tarpan, this horse at Frankfurt Zoo is a much discussed animal.

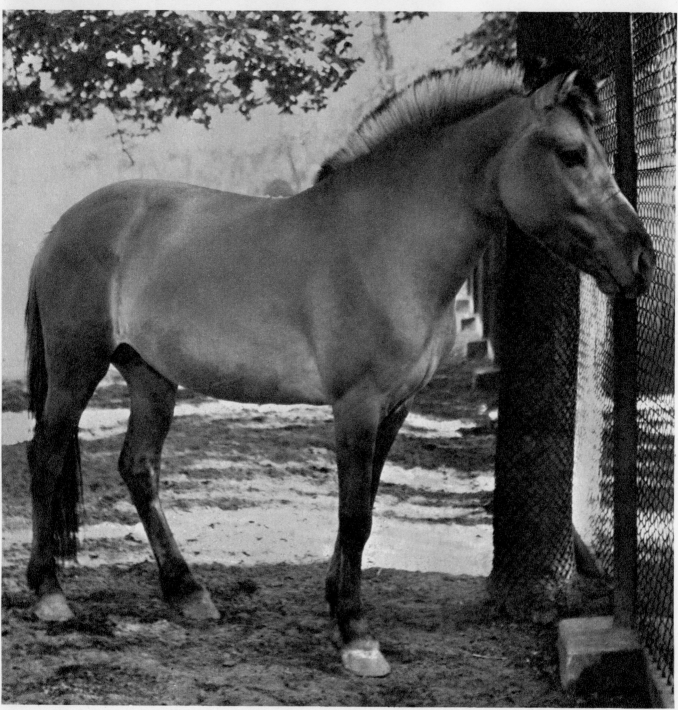

animals. The presence of stripes in most wild horses has caused some people to suggest that the ancestors of the true horses were striped, although this is something which cannot be inferred from the fossils.

Man's first relationship with the horse was as a hunter. His success may be seen at many places, as for example the horse hunters' camp at Solutré in southern France, where it has been estimated that the skeletons of more than 10,000 horses lie among the debris of food remains. It was not until very much later that any domestication took place. Probably donkeys and onagers, one of the half asses, were domesticated first; there are very ancient illustrations from Egypt and Sumeria showing these distinctive animals. Later true horses were domesticated, probably by nomadic tribesmen in Central Asia, possibly as far back as 2500 BC, although the exact time and place is not certain. Their docility and their strength caused them to be favoured above the intractable onagers, and their speed over the donkeys. For a long time horses were the animals of war, and were chiefly used for pulling chariots. Riding was not invented until very much later, perhaps because of the small size of the wild horses. When bigger breeds were developed riding became a possibility, although for a long time no saddles were used, and stirrups are a relatively recent invention. The only horse-like animals never to have been domesticated were the zebras, although during the last century a few were used to

Four Przewalski horses at Hellabrunn Zoo.

An unnamed, wild Mongolian horse which has given birth to a foal in Munich Zoo. When this photograph was taken the foal was only 3 hours old.

pull lightweight carriages.

All domestic horses and ponies of the present day are descended from different forms of the European and Asiatic wild horse. Selection for size, conformation and colour has given us breeds from ponies to thoroughbreds and shire horses. Just how many forms of the one species of wild horse went into the making of our horses is unknown, but it is probable that the tarpan, the subspecies from West Central Asia, was the chief ancestor, with some admixture from Przewalski's horse of North-East Asia, and possibly, a larger, wooded country horse from Europe contributing the stock which led to the development of big breeds at a very early date. Apart from changes in size and colour, one of the differences which seems

to have developed in all domestic true horses, is in the form of the mane, which is erect in wild horses, but falls over the neck in domestic breeds. This change, and others in the structure of the vertebrae are probably to be correlated with a difference in chromosome number between Przewalski's horse and the domestic breeds.

Man has nearly exterminated all of the wild horses except the zebra. The tarpan is now completely extinct, as are most of the forms of the asses and half asses. The reason for this is that the wild horses were all capable of interbreeding with the domestic ones. Wild stallions would abduct the tame mares, and the foals born of their mating were wilder and less useful than fully domesticated horses. Also the

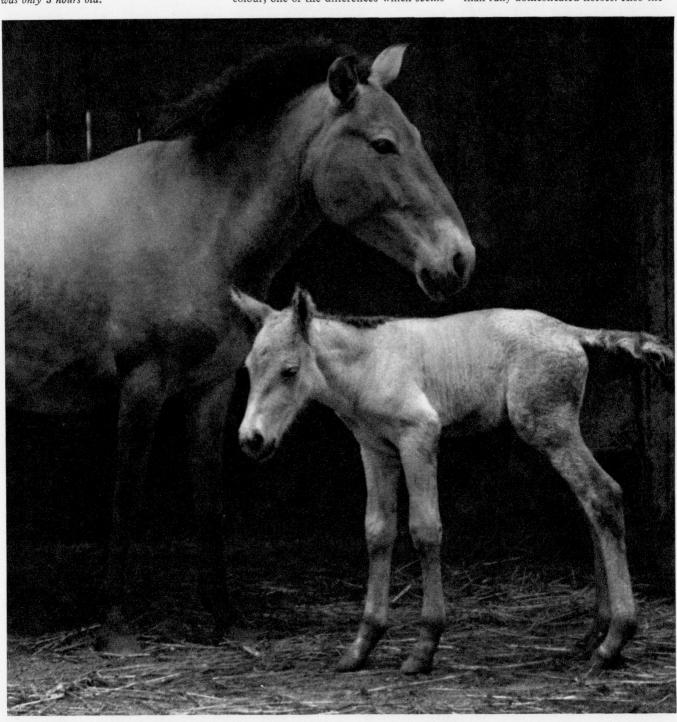

wild horses often damaged crops, and although in many places domestic horse-flesh has always been taboo, wild horses were hunted for food like any other game animal.

Although man has decimated the wild horses, he has taken his domestic animals with him over the world. In some places these have escaped and flourished. Horses of this kind are known as feral animals, rather than wild ones, since they are descended from once domesticated ancestors. The 'wild' horses of the Americas and Australia, are all feral, as are the ponies which have developed in the remoter parts of Britain. However untamed they may be, their structure tells us that they come from stock which was at one time modified by man.

A fine specimen of an Anglo-Arab horse.

Show Jumping

by Dorian Williams

Few sports have become popular quite so quickly as show jumping has since the last war.

It is often suggested that this is due to television. It is true that television has brought show jumping to a huge public that before the war had scarcely heard of it, but I have no doubt in my own mind that without the successes of our riders over the years no amount of television could have made the sport interesting to the layman.

Every sport needs personalities. More, a sport needs names that are famous internationally because of international successes, and this is just what our riders have provided over the years.

It was in 1952 that Britain won the gold medal at the Helsinki Olympics. Riders such as Colonel Harry Llewellyn, Wilf White, Peter Robeson and Pat Smythe with their famous horses Foxhunter, Nizefela, Craven A, Tosca, had already been winning consistently all over Europe since the 1948 Olympics in London. Consequently they started favourites in Helsinki, but they were still comparatively unknown to the British public.

The gold medal changed all that. The medal for show jumping being the only medal of any sort won by a British performer at Helsinki — and that in the very last event of the Games — they came home to a hero's welcome.

Suddenly the name Foxhunter was on everybody's lips. The B.B.C. went for show jumping in a big way. As a sport it was always ideally suited to the medium. Now there were the big names: the personalities that made it important to the viewer that this rider had a clear round, that that rider beat the clock, that the British team won.

Attendances at the big shows increased enormously. The Horse of the Year Show that had started almost disastrously only three years earlier, and nearly folded, suddenly became a sell-out.

As can so easily happen the success of our riders helped the television while the television helped our riders. The one stimulated the other. The greater popularity of the sport resulted in bigger prize money. Bigger prize money made horses more valuable. The greater value of the top horses meant that the top

Caroline Bradley riding Graciano at the Bath and West Show 1968.

Mexico Olympics. Prince Philip congratulating silver medallist Marion Coakes and her mount Stroller.

Marion Coakes (silver), Bill Steinkraus (gold) and David Broome (bronze) winners of the 1968 Olympic Grand Prix individual jumping competition.

(Below) Alan Oliver rides John Glenn at the Aldershot Show.

(Right) Marion Coakes on Stroller taking an obstacle at the Mexico Olympics.

riders and owners could sell off their lesser lights and buy even better horses.

More money was available to send teams abroad, and as in any sport international competition is far and away the most effective training method for big international events.

Britain's international record over the years clearly substantiates this. No other nation has the Olympic record that Britain has: a medal in every Games since the war. A team bronze in London, 1948; a team gold in Helsinki, in 1952; a team bronze in Stockholm, in 1956: an individual bronze — David Broome on Sunsalve — in Rome, 1960; an individual bronze — Peter Robeson on Firecrest — in Tokyo, 1964; an individual silver — Marion Coakes on Stroller — and an individual

bronze — David Broome on Mister Softee — in Mexico, 1968.

Pat Smythe was the first lady rider ever to win a team medal in the Olympics — Stockholm 1956; and Marion Coakes the first lady rider ever to win an individual medal.

In addition to all this, twice in the three years of its existence Britain has won the President's Cup, virtually the World Championship, awarded to the Nation winning the most points in team events.

Obviously Britain's great advantage in this particular event lies in the fact that Britain has a quite remarkable reservoir of riders, particularly young riders. During the last few years often as many as sixteen or eighteen different riders have represented Britain in international events.

This enables two or even three representative teams to be competing abroad at the same time.

That British riders dominated the 1968 Olympic Games cannot be denied, despite the unfortunate incident which befell Marion Coakes and Stroller. Winning both the silver and the bronze in the individual and David Broome being second best individual in the team event was a remarkable record. There was no unfairness or particular bad luck leading to Stroller's elimination, but there is no doubt that if the course for the team event had been no more difficult than the course for the individual event, then it would have presented no problems for Stroller, and Britain would almost certainly have won the team gold.

(Below) Against the background of the burning Olympic flame David Broome takes a jump on Mister Softee.

(Right) David Broome brings Beethoven down the 10ft 6in Derby Bank at Hickstead.

(Bottom right) Mrs Lorna Johnstone of Great Britain participating in the Dressage competition at the 1968 Olympics.

That the course proved to be more difficult was almost entirely due to the ground being quite unexpectedly dead and sticky, which resulted in its giving no help to the horses at all, no spring, so that fences and distances were, from a jumping point of view, vital inches greater. Obviously this was to the disadvantage of the smaller animal.

Nevertheless, despite this failure both the horses and riders of the British team were highly thought of, and it was nowhere disputed that the British team was certainly one of the three greatest in the world, if not the greatest.

But how long can this last? How long can British teams, British riders and horses maintain their superiority?

The competition is certainly hotter every year, but there are other problems. The value of a top-class jumper is so great to-day that it is a great temptation to the owner of one to sell it, usually to a foreign country where show jumping is subsidized by the Government.

Furthermore, show jumping being an expensive sport, our top owners have to win all they can of the good, but by no means spectacular prize money. (To ensure that as many owners as possible benefit, the rules insist that only one third of the total prize money goes to the winner, and that there must be one prize in cash for every five competitors).

This understandable chasing of prize money — less than 20 out 5,000 competitors win more than £1,000 per year — means that there is a tendency in Britain for horses to be overjumped. This can result either in horses becoming stale or tired, or their jumping life being shortened. It was interesting therefore that the Canadian horse, Immigrant, that did so well in Mexico, was only competing in his 10th show.

That these problems will be overcome I have little doubt. Sir Michael Ansell who was the architect of Britain's emergence in the world of show jumping twenty years ago is still at the helm: and he has always firmly stated that the success and survival of show jumping as a popular spectator sport and a viable sport for those participating depends entirely on international success.

Bill Steinkraus of the U.S.A., who won the
gold medal, taking Snowbound over a jump
during the Olympic Grand Prix in Mexico.

(Below) *Mrs Fox-Pitt riding True Flash at the Badminton Horse Trials.*

Alan Oliver riding Fair Play at the Ascot Jumping Show 1966.

David Broome on Mister Softee clearing a fence in style.

Bill Steinkraus on Snowbound in action during the Mexico Olympics.

(Above) Marion Coakes riding Stroller at Hickstead and Mexico.

Lorna Sutherland jumping Popadom out of the lake at the Badminton Horse Trials.

Accidents will happen even at the Royal International Horse Show — Diana Conolly-Carew on Barrymore.

Mr Z. S. Clarke's Sport was the cob of the year at the 1967 Horse of the Year Show.

Three of the smallest horses in the world.

A rarely seen zebroid in Kenya — a cross between a zebra and a horse.

Zebroids being used as pack animals on the lower slopes of Mount Kenya.

(Left) This bareback rider from Australia is obviously about to bite the dust.

The bareback bronc rider holds the rigging with his right hand and maintains his balance by holding his left arm aloft, keeping his legs forward over the shoulders of the horse.

Horses
and
Armour

by Antony Carter

The horse has always been man's most valued companion in the art of warfare, adding to his skills the horse's own speed, mobility and weight. The feudal system of the Middle Ages with its origins in Charlemagne's great empire saw the mounted man-at-arms develop into the heavily armoured knight of noble birth, who formed the elite shock troops of European armies. The knight in armour continued to provide the backbone of an army until the advent of large bodies of professional mercenaries ended the era of chivalry and its rigid codes of honour and courtly love. These professional Swiss and German soldiers with their long pikes began to prove their superiority in battle. Towards the end of the sixteenth century the armoured knight finally lost his dominance to the lighter armed German Reiter who carried a pair of wheel lock pistols. Armed thus and on agile horses unencumbered by armour they destroyed the feudal aristocracy. Lighter armoured but better armed cavalry superseded the knights, until only the Dragoons of the nineteenth century continued to wear a breast plate and backplate, while Lancers and Hussars wore only their flamboyant uniforms. In spite of the degeneration of the knight, the regimented and disciplined cavalry continued to attract the most aristocratic and dashing officers to form an elite force, and the horse continued as man's favoured adjunct of combat until the advent of barbed wire, machine guns and tanks in this century. As the importance of armour in battle rose and fell man's ingenuity to protect himself with a covering of leather, mail and plate armour was used to protect his most important possession, his horse, for without him the knight lost most of his superiority over the common foot soldier.

In Europe before the growth of Charlemagne's empire the foot soldier remained the most important member of an army. The Greek hoplites, fighting in a wedge-shaped formation, the phalanx, proved themselves the most efficient fighting force in the known world. Their superiority, like that of the Roman legions was based on their superb training and discipline in battle. These armies of trained infantry defeated again and again ill-disciplined hordes of cavalry and mounted tribesmen. Even the well armed chariots and the light cavalry of the Persians were defeated by the Greek and Macedonian infantry. Alexander the Great used a strong cavalry arm in his battles that led him into India, but these men rode unarmoured horses which had to march great distances in the heat. The Romans concentrated their strength in their legions, giving their cavalry a less esteemed, secondary role. Consequently while this method of warfare was more than adequate against barbarians it led them into a crushing defeat when faced with Hannibal's more mobile Carthaginian army at Cannae in 216 BC.

While the Roman empire crumbled the horse soldier grew in importance. The legions, often composed of mercenaries with little real will to fight, were defeated by marauding bands of cavalry. Gradually, the ancient civilizations were conquered by well armed, agile horsemen. The Goths conquered Italy, the Vandals sacked Carthage and the Sassennides from Persia attacked the Roman empire's eastern provinces. The legions had lost their discipline while the empire was torn by internal strife, and with them died the age of the heavily armed foot soldier.

Amongst the invaders, the Sassenides armed their horses of the heavy cavalry. The Persians were the greatest armourers in the East, unsurpassed by any in their skill and attention to detail. The ancient Assyrians had protected their horses with a felt covering which saved them from superficial wounds but the Persians developed their armour to perfection, utilizing leather, wood, bronze, copper, plate steel and mail to give their mounts complete protection. Examples of horse armour have been found which were used by the Greeks and the Sarmatian cavalry serving throughout the Roman empire, but the Persians were the first nation to protect their horses for more than a minority. When Xerxes' enormous army invaded Greece in 480 BC a few of the elite cavalry are believed to have protected their mounts with chamfrons, or head pieces, shoulder plates and breast plates. Soon complete armour developed for the

A German chamfron designed to protect the face of a horse of the early sixteenth century. (Tower of London Armoury)

(Far left) A complete matching war harness for both man and horse. Late fifteenth century. The plates of steel of the horse armour were designed to deflect a lance or pike but offered little protection to the underside of the horse. (Wallace Collection)

horse with a chamfron of leather or metal naturalistically formed. The body armour was composed of leather or metal lamellae, or splints, held together by thongs which gave it some suppleness. By the second century AD some horses were protected by long trappers which reached to the knees but were left open at the front and back to allow free movement of the legs. This armour of scales protected the horse's neck while a chamfron covered its face. A lighter armour could be used which left the horse's flanks bare, giving it complete protection from frontal attack. Different types of horse armour continued in production simultaneously. By the fifteenth century armour of mail was in use together with lamellar armour formed by horizontal strips of iron, either mounted on leather straps or joined by mail, both of which gave the armour flexibility. This method, combined with a plate chamfron, gave the horse complete protection down to its knees. Armour gradually lightened until it died out by the beginning of the seventeenth century. Steel was replaced by leather often in large plates which were richly ornamented, but often the only protection was from padded fabric decorated by studs. At the same time man's own armour grew lighter as the developments in warfare made heavy defensive armour an anachronism.

In Europe horse armour was slower to develop and even at its zenith the feudal system insured that it remained a luxury confined to the nobility. As this system of rule established itself throughout western Europe the power of the feudal lord grew in importance. He held sway over his domain with absolute rights over his serfs, owing allegiance only to his king, who would call upon his aid in times of national crises. The lord, surrounded by his knights and squires, formed the well equipped cavalry, while the troops were his own men-at-arms, supplemented by the peasants who were required to arm themselves at his bidding. Armies were composed of extravagantly armed knights backed by the foot soldiers, who remained in a defensive role supporting the cavalry in battle. While the knights armoured themselves their horses remained uncovered until the twelfth century. The men-at-arms wore helmets and mail hauberks, which sometimes only covered their shoulders but could reach to the knees, while they carried a variety of weapons including the spear, sword or halberd, which was a polearm, its iron head combining an axe, spear and hook.

At this time heraldry developed into a universal form of identification on the battlefield. In the twelfth century the man-at-arms wore a silk or linen tunic over his hauberk often emblazoned with his lord's arms or device. Similarly the horses were covered with a cloth apron of silk or velvet which reached to the hooves. It was made in two separate parts and while one part covered the horse's head, chest and forequarters, the other enveloped the rest of its body leaving an opening

for its tail. By the fourteenth century some of these coverings, called a pair of bards, were formed of mail, which gave the same protection to the horse as the knight's mail hauberk. The padded cloth bards were covered by mail or occasionally iron plates, which in the case of mail completely protected the horse. As the knight found that a strong closed helmet was needed to protect his head from sword and lance thrusts a chamfron of stiffened leather, iron or steel was made to cover the horse's head which was then tied over the cloth or mail covering. As armour developed the chamfron became more naturalistically formed. It was made with pieces to protect the ears and eyes and embellished with decoration. Some had a spike attached to the forehead which gave the horse an offensive arm.

By about 1300 a simpler form of protective covering had come into use which remained popular until the seventeenth century. This consisted of leather straps crossing the horse's body, including its chest and neck. These straps

A magnificent set of light horse armour and matching armour for the knight. Such armour would allow freedom of movement for the horse but limited protection for close quarter fighting. The knight would need to depend on his fighting skill to protect both himself and the horse. (Tower of London Armoury)

were often reinforced by metal plates attached to the leather which, while useless against a thrust, offered a relatively cheap protection against sword cuts. This armour, used widely in the fourteenth century wars between England and France, proved inadequate against foot soldiers. English longbowmen defeated the French nobility at Agincourt, 1314, and Crécy, 1346, often destroying their mounts and leaving the armoured knights either stunned or sluggishly fighting off the agile foot soldiers. At the battle of Coutrai in 1302 the French knights were defeated by Flemish townspeople who hamstrung the horses and pulled the nobles from their saddles. In order to protect themselves especially from longbowmen plate armour for both man and horse developed. The knight's mail hauberk reinforced by plate gave way to complete suits of plate armour shaped to deflect an arrow and overlapped to avoid penetration.

By the middle of the fifteenth century the first full armour, or bard, for a horse appeared. This bard, made in Milan, covered the horse's body with large sheets of plate armour riveted together, with a gap for the saddle, and it reached down level with the horse's belly. The neck was encased in flexible iron plates while the head was covered with a chamfron, which included eye and ear guards. These fifteenth century horse armours were the most complete bards made in Europe. They still left the horse's belly and legs uncovered but the belly could only be injured at close quarters, when it was hoped the knight could defend both himself and his mount. Arming the legs was a problem which defeated the great majority of armourers, since it would have impeded the horse. The complete armour therefore included the chamfron for the head, the crinet to protect the neck, the peytral or breast plate, the flanchard which covered the flanks and finally the crupper that guarded the hindquarters. By this period heavier and sturdier horses were being used as cavalry mounts and they were always stallions since no knight would have ridden a mare in combat.

During the sixteenth century full armour as described became universally popular, but already the power of the knights charging in serried ranks, lances lowered, was becoming ousted on the battlefield by the professional foot soldiers. By the end of the century the crinet had become lighter, protecting only the back of the neck, while the throat was protected by leather straps or left unguarded. The sixteenth century saw the introduction of firearms used in quantity in battle, but the knights obstinately hung on to their former glory, entering battle in full armour, which was elaborately decorated or covered by silk covers, embroidered with their arms.

In the last half of the sixteenth century the French knights fought in the Reformation's religious wars. This aristocratic elite entered the battlefield against the German Reiter. These professional soldiers, fighting for the Protestant cause, were armed with a pair of wheel-lock, long-barrelled pistols. They often wore no armour at all and approached the French knights in a rectangle at walking pace, breaking into a canter as they neared, and firing both pistols into the knights at close quarters. As they wheeled to the side to reform and reload another wave attacked the heavily armed French to discharge their pistols into the proud shambles. The era of the sword and lance was over, destroyed by the wheel-lock pistol.

Horse armour with that of the knight degenerated into parade armour which became more ornate and richly decorated. On the battlefield the Cuirassiers became the elite troops, replacing the knights.

These men wore armour protecting their chest and back, thighs and knees, and either a closed or an open helmet guarding the head, neck and cheeks. By the end of the sixteenth century these troops, armed with pistols and a sword, ruled the battlefields of Europe. By the eighteenth and nineteenth centuries only the heavy cavalry continued to wear back and breast plate with a helmet. Horses relied on their speed and agility, coupled with the skill of their riders for protection.

The heavily armed knight and horse were supreme against similarly armed adversaries, but the arrival of armies of mercenaries threatened and finally destroyed their superiority. Against English longbowmen, Flemish burghers,

Heavier armour which gave much more protection to the flanks of the horse, necessitating the use of extra long spurs in order to reach under the armour to spur the horse. (Tower of London Armoury)

Swiss pikemen, German Lansquenets and Reiters they met bodies of soldiers on foot and on horseback, who owed their lives to their skills in fighting as an army, utilizing the most efficient weapons and armour available. The knight's belief in his traditional virtues, based on the medieval code of chivalry which was designed for personal combat, made him a proud figure, but an anachronism in an age when wars were fought by nations and not by the aristocracy alone.

While the knight grew obsolete the horse continued to carry men into battle. Only thirty years ago Polish lancers went into battle against tanks, and German and Russian cavalry struggled together across the Eastern front.

Armour of Charles V of Germany and Spain.

Horse armour known as the 'Burgundian Bard', embossed with the crosses and firesteels of the Order of the Golden Fleece. Probably Flemish, about 1500.

Chamfron and crinet (a flexible neck cover) of Italian design, mid 16th century.

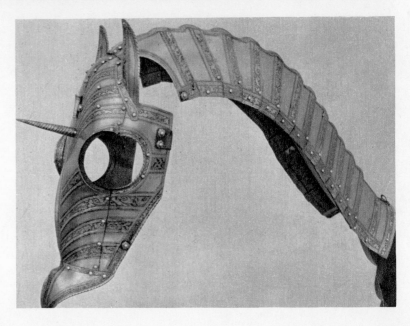

45

The 'gardiens' of the Camargue break
semi-wild horses, which besides being ridden
by tourists are also used for rounding up
cattle.

*Horsa and Hengist, two heavy horses
exhibited by Whitbread Brewery at the
Horse of the Year Show.*

(Left) Rounding up the bulls in the Camargue.

(Below left) To avoid strained tendons, Liberty Horses are not worked on their hind legs until they are mature.

(Below) A goalkeeper's nightmare.

Sibiriak, showing its frightening teeth. This Russian horse bit one of its grooms, who had then to be rushed to hospital.

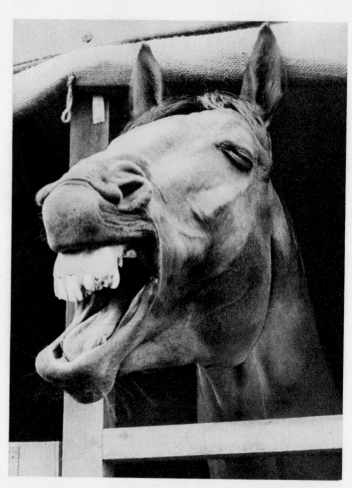

The chair fence is one of the toughest on the notoriously difficult Grand National course.

Early fallers in the 1968 Grand National.

A string of racehorses at exercise on Newmarket Heath.

Four Great Racehorses

by David Wilson

Arkle

Many racehorses are called great, often before they have justly earned such high praise, but there can be no disputing the greatness of these four champions: Arkle, Golden Miller, Hyperion and Ribot.

Arkle himself knew he was a great horse and it was a moving sight to see him striding round the paddock, or in front of the stands, with his ears proudly cocked, looking just what he was, a king among horses. Possessed of remarkable intelligence, combined with speed, stamina and phenomenal jumping ability, he was without question the champion steeplechaser of all time.

Until his injury sustained in the King George VI Chase at Kempton Park in December, 1966, Arkle had dominated the steeplechasing world as no horse had ever done before. It has now been announced that he will never race again. To his legion of loyal supporters this was a sad decision, but certainly the correct one. There could have been no worse spectacle than to see this great horse defeated by horses whom, in his heyday, he would have treated like starter's hacks.

Foaled on April 19th, 1957, he was sold as a three-year old at Goff's Sales in August, 1960. Here he was purchased by the Duchess of Westminster, and he was fortunate indeed to come into the possession of such an experienced and knowledgeable owner.

Arkle first appeared on a racecourse on December 9th, 1961, at Mullingar. The going was extremely heavy and in finishing third, running on through tiring horses, Arkle proved that he could stay. Later in the season, when quite unfancied, he won a three mile hurdle race at Navan beating the favourite, his stable companion, Kerforo.

Following his summer's rest, he re-appeared with an impressive six-length victory in a Handicap Hurdle at Dundalk. This race was the first in a series of nine successive victories each being gained by a wide margin. It was at this point in his career that Arkle first revealed his amazing powers of acceleration.

While Arkle was building up his reputation in Ireland, a young horse named Mill House was establishing himself as a star in England. Two days after Arkle's twenty-length victory in the Broadway Chase at Cheltenham, Mill House was to win the Cheltenham Gold Cup, the steeplechasers' championship. Inevitably, these two great horses were destined to meet in a series of action-packed contests.

Their first meeting was at Newbury in the Hennessy Gold Cup. The race was developing into a thrilling battle when, at the third last fence, Arkle, standing far back and putting in a superlative leap, slipped on landing and was stopped in his tracks. This left Mill House out on his own and he went on to record a comfortable victory. This was a most unsatisfactory outcome, and there was considerable argument as to what would have happened had Arkle run on.

The eagerly awaited return match was in the Cheltenham Gold Cup three months later. This time the Irish were confident that Arkle would gain his revenge. These two great horses dominated the race and coming down the hill to the third last fence Mill House led with Arkle gradually closing the gap. At the second last Mill House was only just in front, and rounding the bend he could find no more. Arkle forged ahead and galloped up the hill to the roar of his vociferous Irish supporters.

Following this great victory, Arkle went on to record twelve more successes, including two more Cheltenham Gold Cups. In many of these races he was giving away two stone and more to good class handicap steeplechasers; horses good enough to carry top weight themselves, had Arkle been absent from the race. Such was the measure of his greatness.

Altogether Arkle ran 35 times, winning 27 races, being second twice, third three times, fourth twice and once unplaced. He amassed a total of £75,107 3s. in prize money, a sum which stands as a record under National Hunt Rules.

Ireland's great steeplechaser in action.

*Arkle ridden by Pat Taaffe at Newbury
where he won the Hennessy Gold Cup
in 1965.*

Arkle, thought by many to be the greatest of all steeplechasers, was forced into premature retirement following a foot injury.

(Below left) Pat Taaffe on Arkle cantering to the start of the Hennessy Gold Cup.

(Below) Taking the jump at a race in Norfolk.

Ploughing on a cold day in Cheshire.

A fine horse and decorated caravan on their way to Appleby Horse Fair.

(Below) Flighty Miss and her mother Firefly.

(Below right) The horse can attain a speed of up to about 30 m.p.h. when racing.

Althea Rodger-Smith on Havana Royal taking a fence at Hickstead.

C. Maizard of France on Orphie at the British Jumping Derby at Hickstead.

A tussle at a Polo match.

A mother and foal of Arab stock grazing near Lake Windermere.

*A very valuable foal by Hyperion, the
stallion of the century, with its mother Djece.*

Golden Miller

The only horse ever to win five Gold Cups and the only horse to win a Gold Cup and a Grand National in the same year, Golden Miller earned an immortal reputation as the greatest steeplechaser of all time. Owned by Miss Dorothy Paget, one of the genuine eccentrics of the Turf, Golden Miller was trained by Basil Briscoe.

Bred in Ireland, Golden Miller changed hands twice before being purchased by Briscoe for 500 guineas. Briscoe had owned a bay gelding named May Crescent who was out of Golden Miller's dam, Miller's Pride. May Crescent had been a faithful servant to Briscoe and so he resolved to look out for any further produce of Miller's Pride. Thus he came by Golden Miller.

Golden Miller's first racecourse appearance was at Southwell, a small Midlands racecourse, and he ran deplorably. In despair Briscoe decided to hunt the horse but this too proved a fruitless venture, as he would not jump the fences correctly, and worse still, he seemed too slow to keep up with hounds.

However, after an enforced rest due to a tendon injury, Golden Miller made rapid improvement. He was third in a handicap hurdle race at Newbury, beaten by much more experienced horses. He then won novices' hurdle races at Leicester and Nottingham and finished second in a steeplechase at Newbury. Shortly after this, due to the illness of his owner Mr. Philip Carr, Golden Miller was sold to Miss Paget for 6,000 guineas.

Following this purchase by Miss Paget he won the 1932 and 1933 Cheltenham Gold Cups, this race being the unquestioned championship of the steeplechasing year.

In 1934 Golden Miller came into his own. He won the Gold Cup easily and just over two weeks later he won the Grand National in record time, carrying the crushing weight of 12st 2lbs.

The following year, 1935, he won what many people consider to be the greatest race run for the Gold Cup. His principle opponent was a little horse named Thomond II. The ground was hard that spring, conditions which favoured Thomond II but were against Golden Miller. A fast pace was set by Southern Hero, a useful horse himself, for the first three miles and when he fell back beaten, Thomond II and Golden Miller came on. Over the second last fence there was little in it, and they were level crossing the last. Thomond II landed with a fractional advantage and ran on gamely, but when the winning post was reached, his rival's great stride had begun to tell and Golden Miller hung on to win by three-quarters of a length.

In 1936 Golden Miller again won the Gold Cup and would no doubt have done so in 1937 had the meeting not been abandoned due to snow on the course.

In 1938, at eleven years of age, Golden Miller attempted to win his sixth Gold Cup. Alas, the years had taken their toll, and gallantly though he struggled, he was beaten by the two years younger Morse Code. It was the first and only time Golden Miller was beaten at Cheltenham. He lost nothing in defeat but the race. His faithful supporters cheered him to the echo as he was led into the stall reserved for the second horse.

Golden Miller ran in 55 races, winning 29 and being placed 13 times. He spent an honourable retirement at his owner's stud in Hertfordshire until he was finally put down in 1957 at the ripe old age of 30

Golden Miller hot on the heels of Morse Code during the 1938 Gold Cup at Cheltenham.

*An earlier picture of Golden Miller, with
E. Williams up, taken in 1937.*

Hyperion

The tiny Hyperion seen here with Tommy Weston measured only 15.2½ hands high.

A son of the Triple Crown winner Gainsborough out of the top class race mare Selene, Hyperion was foaled in April, 1930. As a youngster he was diminutive and even as a mature racehorse he stood only 15.2½ h.h.

As he grew older Hyperion improved in appearance and eventually he was sent along with the other yearlings to Stanley House Stables. Here he was fortunate to come into the charge of the famous trainer, the Hon. George Lambton. Horse and man struck up an ideal relationship and this almost certainly contributed to Hyperion's successes.

As a two-year-old Hyperion was exceptionally lazy and showed no great ability. However, once on a racecourse he adopted a new attitude to life. He began to show off, striding proudly round the paddock and taking a real interest in the proceedings. He had five races as a two-year old, finishing first three times, including one dead-heat, and third twice. His most impressive performance was in the New Stakes at Royal Ascot, which he won by three lengths in the fastest two-year-old time of the meeting.

As a three-year-old Hyperion was lazier than ever, often finishing ten lengths and more behind his galloping companions.

The Chester Vase was chosen for his three-year-old debut and he won the race easily. Hyperion then came to Epsom to run in the Derby as one of Lord Derby's three runners in the race. He started clear favourite and won by a long-looking four lengths, creating what was then a new record time of two minutes thirty-four seconds. This gave an indication of Hyperion's true ability. Following this victory he won the Prince of Wales' Stakes at Ascot. He was then rested prior to being prepared for the St. Leger at Doncaster. Here he proved himself a great horse by making all the running to win easily by three lengths.

Hyperion changed trainers as a four-year-old, and it is almost certain that this affected him, as by now he had come to know Mr. Lambton so well. He won two minor races, by narrow margins, before tackling his principal objective, the Ascot Gold Cup. His jockey Weston considered the horse had been inadequately prepared for the race, and in the event he could only finish third behind Felicitation. He ran once more in a handicap at Newmarket, where he was again beaten.

If his last season racing was disappointing, his success at stud was nothing short of fantastic. Without question he has had the greatest influence on the supremacy of the British Thoroughbred. There is no stud book in the world which does not include a son or daughter of his in their records.

The 4-year-old Ribot winning the King George VI and Queen Elizabeth Stakes in 1956.

Ribot

Ribot after winning the classic of French racing, the Prix de l'Arc de Triomphe, at Longchamp in 1956.

A foal of 1952, Ribot was bred by the great Italian breeder Federico Tesio, and is by Tenerani out of Romanella by El Greco. Federico Tesio, renowned for his genius as a breeder, dearly loved a great horse, especially one bred by himself. It was therefore a great tragedy that Tesio did not live to witness the fantastic performances of Ribot, who is widely considered to be the racehorse of the century.

As a foal Ribot was rather small and for this reason he was not entered in the Italian Classics. This proved to be an unfortunate omission as his racing record will show.

Ribot's racing career is fairly well known. He was unbeaten in sixteen starts over three consecutive seasons in three countries. Thirteen of these victories came in his native Italy, two in France and one in England.

As a two-year-old he won his only three races in Italy. He was again unbeaten as a three-year-old, ending his three-year-old career by beating a field of twenty-three, high-class horses in the Prix de l'Arc de Triomphe in Paris. As a four-year old he was again unbeaten in Italy prior to coming to England to win the King George VI and Queen Elizabeth Stakes. Following this victory he returned to his native Italy to prepare for another tilt at the Prix de l'Arc de Triomphe, the classic of French racing.

He proceeded to win this race in devastating style and it was this second, and farewell victory in the Prix de l'Arc de Triomphe that set a seal upon his brilliant unbeaten career of sixteen consecutive races. Ribot's superb speed was combined with stamina, which made him invincible.

Ribot commenced his stud career in 1957 at Lord Derby's Woodland Stud in Newmarket. At the end of that season he returned to his birthplace, the Dormello Stud. In 1960 he was leased to America for five years for the sum of $1,500,000 and stands at the Darby Dan Stud Farm in Lexington, Kentucky. In every year since he commenced stud duties he has sired a champion.

A truly great horse, he remains a living testimonial to the genius of Tesio.

One of the finest displays of riding that has ever been executed is here seen in the following pictures of the 1968 Derby.

(This page) Lester Piggot on Sir Ivor being led into the unsaddling enclosure after the race.

Lester Piggot (white sleeve bands) on Sir Ivor, seemingly hemmed in, looks as though he has thrown the race away.

The whole field rounding Tattenham Corner, with Lester Piggott in the middle.

Less than a furlong from home with Sandy Barclay on Connaught four lengths ahead, Piggott skilfully pulls Sir Ivor to the outside and takes the lead only 50 yards from the winning post.

Sir Ivor flashing past the post to win the 1968 Derby.

Ponycraft

by Phyllis Hinton

That woolly-bear pony who looks thoughtfully at us through the long hair which falls over his eyes still plays a very important part in the pony world. He gives confidence to the youngest rider, besides teaching him manners and patience, and carries him safely anywhere he chooses to go, whether this is demurely round the block, or over ditches and through convenient places in hedges out hunting.

But his larger and more elegant brother, carefully bred and of great beauty, is perhaps more in the limelight than he is, and the value of this type of pony may well run into several thousands of pounds. Some remain in Britain to breed champion children's riding ponies, or, if crossed with a slightly larger animal of equal merit, to breed hacks to win in the show ring. Others go abroad for the same purpose, or if they are already prize winners over here to compete in countries such as America or South Africa.

Quietly and unobtrusively our ponies have always served us well. Not only have many of our bigger horses been bred from them — and won in every kind of competitive event — but in the dim past there existed only ponies in Britain, sturdy, versatile little fellows who made ideal and extremely handy chariot horses for Boadicea, and whose bones have been found on the ancient camping sites of famous army units, dating back in one instance to AD 79.

Of the mountain and moorland ponies of today — Dartmoor, Welsh, Connemara, Highland, Shetland, Fell, Dales, New Forest and Exmoor — each has its own history and purpose. Some who come straight off the moors and hills to human ownership must face a way of life which to them is incomprehensible. They are asked to carry out inexplicable, unintelligible work, and yet, if not frightened or infuriated, they try to understand and adapt. Many are highly individual and used to fending for themselves in wide, open spaces with the natural surroundings of herbage and streams containing the minerals they need, or on hills and rocky tors which teach them to move well and to become as sure-footed as mountain goats. And they do not lack the companionship of their fellows. Is it any wonder that a pony, which is a herd animal, cannot thrive alone? And that unreasonable treatment, or boredom, or bad riding will turn his naturally quick reactions against instead of for his owner? Freedom they love, and company, and old, inherited instincts are not to be denied.

One very small pony taken from the hills in the Basque country and apparently well settled after a few months in her new home, slipped away in the spring to the land many miles away where she had her first foal, and it was very difficult to find and retrieve her. In those days the running of ponies and brandy over the frontier between France and Spain added spice to an otherwise peaceful life for her, and the sound of these ponies' swiftly moving feet could be heard by those who cared to listen in the night.

And polo ponies. Now, of course, they are usually of the larger, thoroughbred type, ranging from 14.3 h.h. to nearer 16 h.h., but originally, and for quite a while, this fast game was played on, hardy, courageous 13.2 h.h. ponies, until the height limit was officially removed. As Rudyard Kipling tells us in 'The Maltese Cat', perhaps the greatest polo story of all time —'he knew every trick and device of the greatest game in the world and for two seasons had been teaching all the others all he knew or guessed'. The Maltese Cat was, in fact, 'desperately quick on his feet', as well as being the 'Past, Pluperfect, Prestissimo Player of the Game'. Nowadays polo is played by ponies in the New Forest but not with quite the same dedication and élan of the Maltese Cat. New Forest ponies race across country too, and indeed there are quite a few unofficial races in the West of England for all types of ponies, including those with some thoroughbred blood in their veins.

Ponycraft — so much is encompassed in the title as, for example, breeding, handling, schooling and selling, in addition to just ordinary riding and enjoyment. Perhaps the first thing to achieve is an understanding of the pony himself, for without it you will get nowhere. The next is appreciation of the fact that breeding, schooling *and* selling are now highly specialized and must be learnt the right way. There are many pony studs in Great Britain and elsewhere and the quality of the good ones is always reflected in their ponies. These may be mischievous, and have considerable individuality of character, but they will look well and they won't be afraid — or spiteful.

At many studs the stallions run free for a part of the year, at others they are ridden regularly and not kept shut in. Natural surroundings, good feeding, reasonable handling and the correct choice of sires and dams all lead to success, but patience is always important as no stud is built up, or gains a name in a short time. The requisite know-how may take many years to acquire but when it really is attained the market for the right type of pony is wide open, and so is the price. The less good pony who is, in fact, a very sound, intelligent and worthwhile animal, but who just lacks that something which adds another nought to the figures on the cheque, is always wanted for the average rider, both child or lightweight adult. All that is needed is that he shall have been well fed as a yearling and onwards throughout his youth, and slowly and intelligently broken at the right age.

That is the breeder's chief problem. Either the ordinary pony will cost him quite a lot of money before he is mature and ready to sell, or he must find a buyer who will purchase a yearling, or two-year-old, turn him out with another pony, feed and care for him and eventually break him when he is three or four. He, the breeder, must also have the right eye to spot in good time which pony to keep for his own purposes and which to sell. Loud and long have been the lamentations of those who sold the wrong one!

Proper training in pony stud work is now as important as any other kind of preparation for a career, and the National Pony Society of Stoke Lodge, 85 Cliddesden Road, Basingstoke, Hampshire, handles inquiries from all over the world and offers diplomas which are a great asset to all those who take the trouble to learn the right way.

Welsh Mountain pony and foal.

Well-groomed Welsh pony.

Pupils are accepted at various studs. But what is there to learn? There is so much that can only be learned by experience and observation coupled with expert advice. Watch the terrific action of the Welsh Mountain pony stallion as he circles the ring, snowy mane and tail flying like banners, swiftness and power implicit in each fast-moving stride, how straight he goes, each limb, each joint working with equal strength and in perfect unison — here is true rhythm, power, impulsion. Only by right breeding, right handling, feeding and understanding of the pony himself can this be achieved — each detail learnt as one learns first the alphabet before progressing to the written word, remembering always, that even if certain fundamentals remain the same each breed is quite different. The breeder must always keep his ultimate objective in mind — does he wish to breed the pure mountain and moorland pony; or the riding pony which results from a judicious cross; or the high class, near-thoroughbred type of children's 14.2 h.h. show pony?

The Arab horse enters the picture at this point. Sometimes he may be of pony size, but he is always looked upon and spoken of as a horse, and he has contributed immeasurably to the quality of our native breeds. The Arab stallion, Naseel, sired the famous champion, Pretty Polly, out of Gipsy Gold — a simple little Welsh mare. Pretty Polly in turn produced the almost more famous Pollyanna, who was sired by the Welsh Bwlch Valentino, and after winning endless championships in Britain, was sold to America for a sum in the region of £6,000, and retrained most successfully to win in performance events over there. No doubt she will eventually crown her career by producing sons and daughters of equal merit — and talent.

Why do we love them so much? Why are they being bred in many different countries as never before in pony history? Not only for commercial or strictly practical reasons are they wanted, but in these complicated times they are simpler, more earthy, perhaps, and yet they make us really think — a change from the impact of the text book. Friends, dear companions, pests, little devils, responsibilities, yes, they are all of these things and yet we would not be without them.

Highland ponies, garrons, and others of the right dimensions take us safely trekking in Scotland over magnificent country we should have missed without their co-operation. All types of Welsh ponies, including the much liked and remarkably strong shepherding pony, carry us on unforgettable holidays in that glorious Principality. Others show us the New Forest, Dartmoor, Exmoor and many other places, all equally beautiful but completely different.

Lesser-known types of pony are still bred in the West of England. The rugged little island of Lundy, belonging to the county of Devon, still has a few ponies of its own and the pony of the Quantock

Hills in Somerset is flourishing. They are of 13.2 h.h. to 14.2 h.h. approximately in height and are rounded up and sold each September, usually about a fortnight before Bridgwater Fair. These ponies have no society to guard their interests, or stud book to record their breeding. Two of the stallions which have run with the mares are Waterfall (he is by an Arab out of a New Forest mare) and Jude, of Arab-Welsh breeding. Their youngsters have turned out very well, good-looking, kind in temperament and excellent to hunt, hack or show. It is believed that a hundred years ago the Quantock ponies were of almost pure Exmoor blood.

Spotted ponies, some white splashed with dramatic black spots, others with 'blanket' markings, which are spots of any colour on a white rump or back, or 'snowflake' (white spots on a foundation of any colour) have always had a certain popularity in Britain and are now being bred in larger numbers than ever before. It is said that about 3,500 years ago, somewhere on the steppes of Asia, they were first domesticated and since then they have spread all over the world.

Perhaps one of the most beautiful of all is the golden, fairy-tale Palomino pony, often referred to in stories and legends. His coat must be the colour of a newly minted sovereign, or no more than three shades darker or lighter, his tail and mane white with nor more than 15% dark or chestnut hairs in either, and his eyes, dark brown, hazel or black iris, and both of the same colour. Quite often this pony is

A New Forest pony foal.

of Welsh breeding and looks very charming when ridden or pulling a light dogcart.

So many ponies are driven in harness today, both singly and in pairs, from gay and busy little Shetlands to hackneys whose speed and dash literally make the wheels spin like tops. One Fell pony I knew not long ago was hacked, hunted and shown in breed classes by a man whose mother drove the pony when she felt like an outing of this description. Another pony is still used by a butcher on his rounds, who also drives him to meets of hounds.

Although ponies in harness are generally well turned out, there is the story of Kitty who until a couple of years worked and lived in a street dealer's yard in Wandsworth, near London, old, worn and with her feet in very bad condition. Meanwhile a man of no experience with horses who, throughout his hardworking life, had longed to own and drive a pony decided that he could at last afford the time and money to do so. He was offered the somewhat derelict Kitty at a handsome price and he bought her believing her to be only eight years old instead of nearer eighteen. But Kitty's lucky star was in the ascendant, and instead of selling her for meat when he learnt about her age and her feet, he set to work unremittingly to get her right and to improve her condition, which, he was told, was shocking. Knowing nothing, he took the trouble to

Alan Oliver on Bay Rum VII at the Greater London Horse Show at Clapham Common.

learn and never flagged in his careful nursing. One day, quite by accident, I saw him driving a trim Kitty to a nicely painted cart in outer London, stopped to congratulate and admire, and advised him to show her in classes for trade turnouts at shows. This he did and the little mare won the highest honours against strong competition. A true story with a happy ending.

Brief Descriptions of the Mountain and Moorland Breeds

The *Dartmoor pony* is usually black, grey, bay or brown in colour. Chestnuts are rare. Piebalds and skewbalds are not accepted. He must not be more than 12.2 h.h. in height. His limbs are remarkably strong, he has good feet and a beautiful little head with prick ears.

The *Exmoor* is very strong and sturdy for his size. Mares must not be more than 12.2 h.h. and stallions 12.3 h.h. The colour is bay, brown or dun, with no white points. These ponies have light, mealy-coloured muzzles and eyelids, and because of the latter they are sometimes described as having a 'toad eye'. All have 'snow tails' i.e. short hairs at the top to prevent snow from clogging at the end.

The *Connemara* was first bred only in Ireland and has made a useful contribution to the breeding of show-jumpers and event horses. There is now a Connemara Society in Britain. The height varies from

A jumping competition at a local show.

13 h.h. to 14.2 h.h., and they are of various colours, but grey seems to be predominant. Versatile and useful they make an excellent 'family pony'.

The *Welsh* pony ranges from the beautiful little Welsh Mountain pony who must not exceed 12 h.h. and can be of any colour except piebald and skewbald, to the larger Welsh cob and pony of cob type. Welsh Section B ponies may reach 13.2 h.h. and have greater substance.

The *New Forest* pony varies considerably in size and type, some being quite small, others reaching 14.2 h.h. Many are very good riding ponies, others also work in harness. They may be of any colour except piebald or skewbald.

The *Fell* and *Dales* ponies are two distinct breeds, though closely related by virtue of the type of work for which they were originally bred i.e. as pack ponies. They carried lead from the Fells to the dockyards. The *Fell* pony ranges from 13 h.h. to 14 h.h., carries himself well and is versatile and intelligent to a degree. The most popular colour is black and there are browns, bays and greys with an occasional dun. The *Dales* are often about 14.2 h.h. and usually black or brown, with a very occasional grey or bay.

Of the larger ponies perhaps the friendly *Highland* is the most spectacular in colour, varying from pure grey to silver-dun, blood-red chestnuts with silver manes and tails, and other delectable shades. Their large, velvety eyes add to their attraction and they can carry considerable weight.

Pony-trekking in the Highlands of Scotland.

A sturdy little foal in a meadow in Germany.

A Fell pony belonging to Her Majesty the Queen.

A very handsome show pony.

Learning to jump
during a Pony Club
meeting.

A very fine pony for
a young rider.

A Pony Club on
a day's trek in
South Wales.

Members of the
Wimbledon Pony
Club riding on
Wimbledon Common.

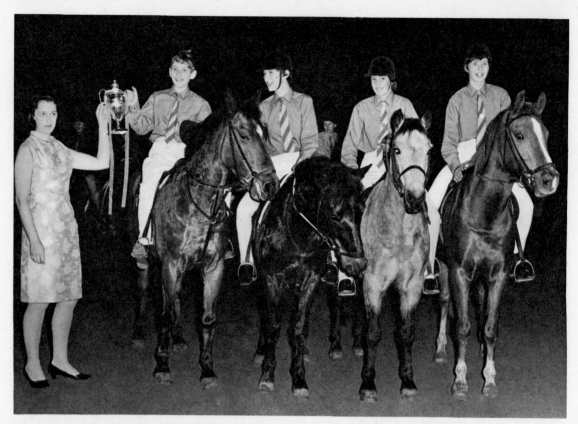

Pony Club teams take part in Mounted Games at the Horse of the Year Show.

Cooling off after a gallop along the sands.

A Norwegian mare
with her foal.

The Horse in Myth and History

by Michael Stapleton

Towards the end of the third millennium BC there was a great irruption of new peoples into the civilized Near East. Great numbers of pastoral nomads from the north made their way to the Iranian plateau, where for a century or so they seemed to pause. Then waves of them swept down from the high ground, some driving into Asia Minor and others to the edge of the fertile valleys of the Tigris and Euphrates. Some went north from the Bosphorus and reached the Danube, while others turned south at Thessaly and made their way into Greece.

By the beginning of the second millennium every settled community was feeling the effects of the movement; it continued for centuries and those who did not resist it — and eventually succumb — fled in front of it and increased the upheaval. It was a time of great change and a point of departure in the story of man.

The newcomers appear in the pages of history under various names: as Hittites, Achaeans, as Medes and Persians; the wave that turned eastwards and entered India are called the Aryans — but this was after they established their identity and entered the world stage. Who they were before that, or how widely they were spread is not known with any degree of certainty. They are described as the Indo-Europeans, and it is believed that their homeland was the grass-covered plains to the north-east of the Caspian Sea. The southward and eastward migrations were paralleled by similar movements north and west; the plains of south Russia were occupied, and the movement continued to the Baltic Sea and beyond. The Sarmatians and Scythians of the steppes are known to history; the farthest travelled ones emerged at a later date as Vikings and Norsemen.

The Indo-Europeans carried all before them. Their apparently savage society was in fact a highly organized one, with a nomad aristocracy in firm control of a submissive pastoral population. They were skilled metal workers and had a formidable weapon which they cast from bronze, a war-axe which they used with annihilating effect. And no empire standing in their way could match their speed and mobility, because the Indo-Europeans had the horse. They were the first people in history to domesticate the animal, and their dependence on it brought it into the world's mythology.

It was not long before other races saw the value of this marvellous creature, which could carry armies, provide flesh to eat and hides to be made into clothing and boots. The Assyrians, those great conquerors of the second millennium, made great use of it; so did the Egyptians, after the Hyksos kings — themselves originally Indo-Europeans who had been allowed to settle in the Nile Delta — demonstrated its value and transformed the methods of Egyptian warfare, paving the way for the glories of the Eighteenth Dynasty. The Egyptians crossed the small Asiatic horses with the more powerful and tractable Arab breed from Libya, and these were the ones a king of Israel was to covet, as we shall see.

The Assyrians have left us superb reliefs showing their kings in horse-drawn chariots. But the Egyptians' representations are of much less interest than their brilliantly rendered bulls, rams, falcons, and the other creatures which played so important a part in their religion. True, the horse was a creature they used, rather than venerated, but one regrets its absence from a great period in art.

But while most of the peoples of antiquity were quick to make use of the horse there was one race — and one from whom Western man derives many of his traditions — who apparently regarded the animal with detestation. These were the Hebrews. That the horse was known to the early Hebrews there is no doubt; the Ras Shamra tablets of about 1800 BC mention them as creatures of great value in the Near East, and the Hebrews entered Egypt about a century later, during the time of the Hyksos kings. The Exodus occurred at a time when the horse was well established in Egypt, during the Eighteenth Dynasty, and it seems curious that a whole nation, at this time, should have migrated on its feet. It may have been that the horse was too valuable a creature for them to acquire — but even this leaves us unprepared for the remarkable strictures uttered by Moses in the Book of Deuteronomy. The context is the appointment of a king over Israel in God's good time (xvii. 16).

'. . . one from among thy brethren shalt thou set king over thee: thou mayest not set a stranger over thee, which is not thy brother. But he shall not multiply horses to himself, nor cause the people to return to Egypt, to the end that he should multiply horses: forasmuch as the Lord hath said unto you, "Ye shall return henceforth no more that way".'

And it is true that of all the people of antiquity the early Hebrews alone resolutely ignored the creature which could have made light of so much of their labour and graced so many of their occasions. They were of course very conscious that the habits of other peoples were displeasing to the Lord, and in the time of Moses horses would have been associated with the hated Egyptians. It has also been suggested that the stricture was provoked by the practice of buying horses with men — of sending them as slaves or to serve as mercenaries in Egypt in exchange for horses. This could only have been done by one in supreme authority, i.e. the king, and it is Solomon who is regarded as the first to indulge in the practice. His extravagance drove him to many strange measures to maintain the luxury of his court and complete the building of the Temple. It was his father, David, who first saw how useful horses would be to a small nation obliged to struggle with more powerful neighbours.

Solomon was the third King of the Jews, and reigned some five centuries after the time of Moses. But since the Book of Deuteronomy, as we know it, was certainly not written at the *time* of Moses it is possible that the stricture may have been fashioned to fit the time of the kings.

Thus it is that so many of our oldest sources of direct history tell us so little about man and his association with the horse. The great civilizations of Egypt, Assyria, Babylon; the matchless language of the Old Testament — none of these have anything to say about the creature that they all, sooner or later, were only too

eager to make use of. It was a creature from elsewhere, of people they regarded with apprehension. And it is to these we must turn to discover how the horse took its place in mythology.

II

When the Aryans entered India they were the bearers of traditions already old. Scholars can only guess at the true age of the *Rig Veda;* the oldest written versions have allusions to Brahmanism that are factually nonsensical in the context, since the Aryan gods of the Vedas bear little relation to Hinduism as it was formulated some time between the eighth and fifth centuries BC. It is loosely said that the *Rig Veda* was composed about the middle of the second millennium BC; that the hymns which form it were brought to India with the Aryans and are probably as old as 2500 B.C. It is agreed at least that the *Rig Veda* is very old indeed and was probably familiar, in an oral version, to the Aryans at the time when the Indo-Europeans began to explore the world that lay beyond the plains of central Asia. Scholars point out that the Persian god Mithra appears in the Vedas as Mitra, an aspect of the sun god; in the Persian pantheon he is the 'genius of Heavenly Light'; that the Vedic sky god has a name very similar to its Greek and Roman equivalent — he is Dyaus, and we have Zeus, Deus, Jove; Dyaus is sometimes called Dyaus-pitar, 'heavenly father', and we also have Jupiter. Athene is likened to Vach, the Vedic goddess who became the Hindu Sarasvati. The Sanskrit, Greek and Latin languages all have an Indo-European root. The common origin of these widely spread traditions is well attested, and those of the greatest antiquity, the Aryan, most clearly show the horse's importance to Indo-European man.

The oldest traditions, i.e. race memories, die hard. The influence of the Brahmins could not disguise the origins of the Vedas, and there is a remarkable survival from former times in the great Hindu epic, the *Mahabharata*. It was written down about the third century BC but is believed to stem from a much earlier epic transmitted by oral means. The Brahmins gave it scriptural status for the Hindus by making their gods take part in much of the action; Vishnu, particularly, is honoured as the divine watcher who intervenes, and Shiva is invoked by one of the heroes who wishes to gain strength. But contained in the Fourteenth Book of the written version is the remarkable episode of the horse sacrifice, the *Aswa-Medha*, remarkable because nowhere in Hindu scripture is the creature honoured. Furthermore, the god concerned in the sacrifice is Indra, the pre-Hindu principal god and a much warmer character than any of the later trinity of Brahma, Vishnu, and Shiva.

The original sacrifice, in Vedic times, was performed by kings to obtain fertility in their marriages and thus ensure the succession. The horse was killed at sunset in the presence of all the king's wives, who had to pass the night by the carcass. Upon the chief wife fell the duty of going through a symbolic coupling with the dead beast. This extraordinary rite, by the time of the *Mahabharata*, had developed into something much more elaborate, and remained the prerogative of kings.

In the *Mahabharata* one of the Pandava brothers, Yudhisthira, after many vicissitudes and exhausting wars, succeeds in gaining the throne from his half-brothers, the Kauravas. In the Fourteenth Book, the *Aswa-medhika-parva*, he duly ascends the throne and consolidates his kingdom by performing the *Aswa-Medha*, the horse sacrifice of the title. This began by the selection of a horse of a particular colour, which was then turned loose to wander at will for the space of a year. The king followed the horse with an army, and was obliged, when the horse wandered into a strange country, to challenge the ruler, who could make up his own mind whether to submit or give battle. Upon the outcome of the year's campaigns depended the prestige of the king: if he returned at the end of the year with a number of vassals in his train he enjoyed a triumph; if on the other hand he came back with no more of an army than when he set out he was regarded with scorn. The horse rode back in the train of the triumphant king, who then sacrificed it to Indra.

It was said that a hundred of these sacrifices would enable a mortal king to overthrow Indra himself and become the ruler of the universe. A safe enough thing to say — there was little likelihood of any king being crowned a hundred times. In the epic, Yudhisthira performs the *Aswa-Medha* with conspicuous success and the Pandavas settle down to a reign of peace and prosperity.

It is remarkable that the *Mahabharata*, with its burden of Brahmanic gloss, should retain this account of a ceremony which plainly looks back to the time when nomad chieftains established their hegemony by the simple method, probably, of demanding of neighbouring chieftains that they yield up their herds and their pastures. The fertility rite already described would probably have followed. The elaboration of these into the *Aswa-Medha* is paralleled in other religions where basically simple rites are commemorated with complicated and costly ceremonies. In some cases we know both the original simple rite and can witness the elaborate ceremony, but the account in the *Mahabharata* points the way back over a seemingly endless road.

The epic was written down in the third century BC, but it was very much older than that. The horse sacrifice described there stems from the Vedic one which sought a fruitful marriage for the king — and how old can that be? If the *Rig Veda* goes back to 2500 BC where lie the origins? Probably at the time when man first domesticated the horse, somewhere in the Asian grasslands, untold centuries ago.

III

In these same grasslands, in the fifth century BC, lay the home of the Massagetae and their queen, Tomyris, who defeated the great Cyrus and abused his corpse on the battlefield. The Massagetae, Herodotus says, worshipped only the sun, and to the sun they sacrificed horses, regarding it as fitting that the fleetest of gods should be offered the fleetest of mortal creatures.

The Persians themselves revered the horse no less than the Massagetae. Their huge white Nesaean horses were regarded as sacred, and children were trained in the mastery of the horse from the age of five. And while they may not have known that the Massagetae were their racial kindred, they were, throughout their history, fascinated by the rolling plains which lay beyond the northern mountains. King Darius tried conclusions with the Scythians, just as Cyrus did with the Massagetae. And he was worsted, too, though he did not die as Cyrus had done.

Neither the Scythians, nor the Sarmatians whose dominion lay farther to the west, have left us an account of their beliefs. Most of what we know comes from Herodotus, and his account of the Scythian kings' burial customs is borne out by the details revealed when the Scythian tombs were excavated. These extraordinary mausoleums were covered with huge mounds of earth after the ceremonies were completed, to merge into the landscape and remain undiscerned until the nineteenth century. When they were uncovered the skeletons of horses and knightly riders were found — just as the Greek historian had described — carefully placed, killed to escort the dead king on his journey into the next world. As many as fifty horses and riders were found in the larger tombs. Herodotus's account of the method of killing a horse for sacrifice — by binding the front legs, throwing the horse, and then strangling the creature with a tourniquet round the neck — was actually witnessed in this century, performed by Siberian shamans.

The mythology of the Greeks abounds with names that point to the importance of the horse in their early history, though the sophisticated formulation of their religion by Hesiod and Homer makes no mention of it. (The invaluable Herodotus has an amusing comment in his *Histories* (Book II) to the effect that the Greeks did not know their gods until the two poets told them who they were and whence they came, i.e. that Hesiod and Homer were the first Greeks to give the gods family trees, assign their functions, and disentangle their various aspects.)
The most familiar are perhaps Hippolyte (the Amazon queen), Hippolytus (the chaste son of Theseus whom Phaedra lusted after), Hippodameia (the wife of Pelops and mother of Atreus), Chrysippus, son of Pelops and Astyoche (loved by Laius, and the indirect reason for the journey that led to the encounter with Oedipus), and Hippasus (the son who was

Horses are often shown in this stylized fashion in Egyptian art whether the subject is a battle, a triumph, or a gazelle hunt as depicted here.

A Hittite relief showing a lion hunt. The horse-drawn chariot transformed the ancient art of war in the Near East.

Representation of a horse on a Persian relief.

torn to pieces by his mother Leucippe — who is also horse-named).

The meaning of the names is as follows: Hippolyte and Hippolytus — 'of the stampeding horses', Hippodameia — 'horse tamer', Chrysippus — 'golden horse', Hippasus — 'horseman', Leucippe — 'white mare'. The winged horse Pegasus is perhaps the most famous horse in mythology; he was beloved of the Muses because he created the spring on Mount Helicon by stamping his hoof. The well is called Hippocrene — 'the horse well'. Robert Graves points out that he stamped his 'moonshaped hoof', and maintains that the pre-Olympian deity of the Greek world was matriarchal and specifically a *moon* and earth goddess. The horse was sacred to her, because with its moon-shaped hooves it played an important part 'in the rain-making ceremonies and the instalment of sacred kings'. This is very close to the *Aswa-Medha* of the Aryans, and the myth of Pegasus in its familiar form makes it clear that the winged horse was sacred to Athene, whom Graves sees as a descendant from the original concept of the pre-Olympian Great Goddess.

This same Great Goddess — the Mother — as the forerunner of an established pantheon was present in the north, where her representatives were associated with magic. H.R. Ellis Davidson points out a direct connection between these womens' practices and the horse cult of the Vanir, the deities whose especial province was the care of the earth and its fruitfulness. The chief goddess of the Vanir was Freyja, and she was promised to the giant who undertook to build a wall round Asgard, the home of the gods. When the wall was nearly finished there were only three days left before spring, and the gods belatedly realized what would happen to the earth if Freyja, the goddess of fertility, was taken from them. The giant relied on his great horse, Svaoilfari, to do half his work for him; the horse was tireless, and worked all through each night. So Loki, the trickster god, took the form of a mare

An early representation of a Centaur. At first Centaurs were shown as men with horses' bodies growing out from the hips. Later the creature became a man only from the waist upwards.

and lured the great horse away. The wall was never completed, Freyja was kept safe, and the union of Svaoilfari with the divine mare produced the finest of all steeds, the eight-legged Sleipnir, who could ride through the air and who became the horse of Odin, the Lord of Hosts, the god of war, and the god of the dead.

The Siberian shaman mentioned earlier would have been much at home with the chief of the Norse gods. The shaman's chief duty lay in maintaining a connection between the living and the dead, and he was always carried to the other world on the back of a horse. For this purpose Odin has Sleipnir, and when his son Hermod offers to go to the world of the dead to try and bring Balder back to life, his father gives him Sleipnir to carry him there.

IV

The story of the horse in mythology is almost the story of the horse and man, and this short account can do little more than show how persistent the cult was among our ancestors. It varied, of course, in different areas, and the changing form of religion over the centuries varied it even more. There is no trace of it in the Greek religion, but Herodotus and Robert Graves show us both that it was there originally, and that the religion was formulated quite late in Greek history. The instalment of the sacred king was a rite that involved the horse there once, just as it did in Vedic India. The ancient Scythians strangled their horses when they sacrificed them, as does the Siberian shaman, who rides a horse to the world of the dead, as Odin rides on Sleipnir. The Scythians buried their horses in great mounds with their dead kings, while the Norsemen sacrificed the enemy's horses after a victory. The connections are so numerous as to make the common origin beyond question, but there is one more interesting enough to merit mention. In the *Eddas* there is the story of the Voluspa, the prophecy which warns Odin of the coming doom of the gods. The story tells, by the way, of a woman who venerated a household god — which was the generative organ of a horse. The Norse housewife had that much in common with the chief wife of the Aryan kings.

References:

Oesterley and Robinson. *A History of Israel*. Vol. I, 1932

Dowson, J. *A Classical Dictionary of Hindu Mythology*. 1961 edition

Graves, Robert. *The Greek Myths*. 2 Vols., 1955

Graves, Robert. *The White Goddess*. 1948

Herodotus. *The Histories*. Translated by Harry Carter. 1962

Ellis Davidson, H.R. *Gods and Myths of Northern Europe*. 1964

Rostovtzeff, M. *Iranians and Greeks in South Russia*. 1922

A relief from the Parthenon showing a contest between a Centaur and a Lapith.

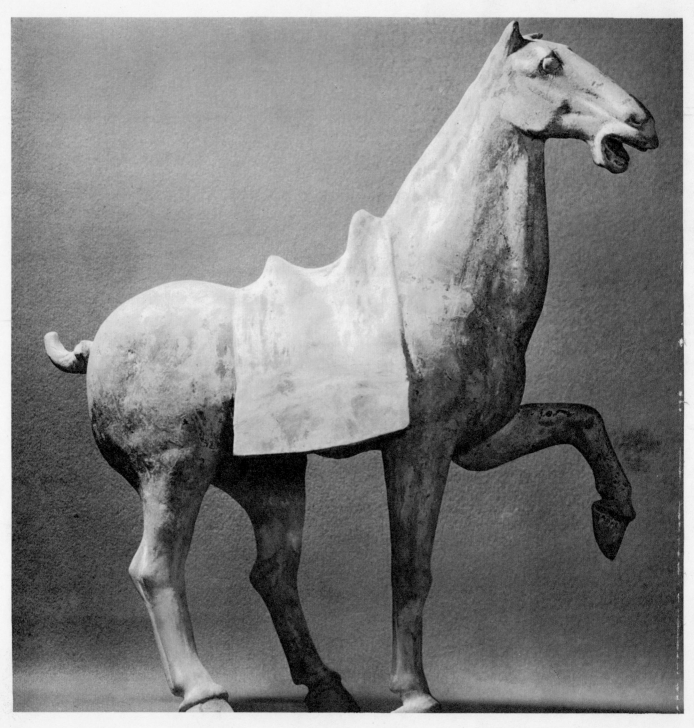

A Chinese Tang Dynasty bronze horse of the 7th—10th century AD.

A bronze figure of a horse and rider from the Greek and Roman Antiquities Department of the British Museum.

Japanese painting of a warrior on horseback,
wiping his sword.

A horse carved from an exceptionally large piece of black and dark grey jade from the Tang Dynasty (618—906 AD).

A display by the Southdown Hunt at a local show in Sussex.

Hunters and Hunting

by E. Hartley-Edwards

God made the Horse,
He made the Hound,
And then, for right good measure,
He made the wily red-backed Fox,
To bring them both together.

Although to the majority of hunting folk the exclusion of the horse from the triumvirate of the chase would be unthinkable, he is, in fact, the least essential. The essence of hunting lies in the availability of a suitable quarry (the best of all and the one most fitted by Nature, being the fox) and the possession of the means to hunt it, which is best supplied by a pack of hounds bred solely for that purpose.

Before the land was enclosed, in the early days of hunting, the devotees of venery followed hounds who hunted steadily throughout the long day at little more than walking pace. In such conditions the fascination of the exercise was in studying, at fairly close quarters, the hounds working up to their quarry, the fact that they were followed on horseback being incidental.

Once the common lands were fenced, however, and it became necessary to jump, there came a period when speed was regarded as the criterion of a good hunt, and it culminated in the enormous, hard-riding fields to be seen in the Shires of the mid-18th century, when the true art of hunting was almost lost in the thunder of hooves and oaths as hundreds of horsemen charged the stout fences of Leicestershire and Northamptonshire.

The thrills of speed and the introduction of the Thoroughbred horse assumed an ascendancy over the quieter and more subtle pleasures contained in witnessing the pursuit of a stout fox by a persevering pack.

It was all very exciting but it had little to do with the *art* of hunting.

The old type of hound, heavy, slow, but possessed of an undeniable nose and having a cry like a peal of bells on a Christmas morning, was replaced by a lighter sort, built for speed, and the foxes, in consequence, had to move a bit quicker, too. The old carriage horse, as able to take his turn at the plough as with hounds, disappeared, his place being

taken by a sort which bore about as much resemblance to him as a 1928 Daimler does to a 1970 E-type Jaguar.

Nevertheless, although a great many men and women hunted for the ride, as is the case today, the essence of hunting remained, and still remains, with the two prime essentials, the quarry and the pack which pursues it.

In our own times many thousands of people have discovered the delights of hunting, without suffering the inconvenience which a horse would seem to constitute for some mounted followers, by following hounds in motor cars, on bicycles and on foot. Even in the Shires there is one assiduous, and one imagines superbly fit, hunting man who, disdaining the sartorial elegance of the mounted contingent for a comfortable sweater and a pair of plimsolls, jogs with hounds from cover to cover, and is by all accounts a hard man to follow when the pack is running.

It is more than possible that those who hunt in this way see a lot more of the actual proceedings than the scarlet-clad gentleman, desperately concerned with restraining his over-fresh hunter as he gallops, half-blinded with flying mud, down a treacherous ride in company with his peers.

For the mounted followers, however, the reasons for hunting remain much the same as when Surtees examined them through the mouth of John Jorrocks, the grocer from Coram Street, whose passion for hunting eclipsed even the considerations of 'a case of prime Tokay'.

'Some,' said that most lovable of fox-hunters, ' 'unt for the ride out, some for the ride 'ome, some to get away from their wives . . .' and so on.

And most, particularly the younger ones, whose number increases from year to year, ' 'unt for the ride'. For them it is in the horse and the riding of him over the country that the joy of fox-hunting lies.

There will, of course, always be the hard-core of men and women of Jorrocks' 'precious few' who hunt for the sake of hunting and to whom the horse is but a means of getting to hounds. And, as time goes on and the ardour of youth is abated, it is possible that the dashing young

The Master drinks his stirrup cup.

thruster of today will join that select band, and find his or her pleasure in the wiles of 'the thief of the world' and the capability of hounds to hunt him down, rather than in the galloping and the jumping of fences, which in truth they could do equally well without benefit of either quarry or pursuers.

Whatever the motivation that prompts people of all ages to go hunting on a horse, the choice of a suitable one is clearly of some importance and will depend to a great extent on the country in which they hunt and the depth of their pockets.

Although, in general, it is true that particular types of horses will be better suited to certain countries than others, just as hounds are bred to fulfil the requirements of the country they hunt in, it is quite surprising how varied an assortment of horses will give good service in as many different conditions.

For hunting over the grass and over big fences nothing can exceed the Thoroughbred horse of scope, with his ability to gallop and jump, but he may well not be a possibility for the owner-groom whose job prevents him hunting except at the weekend. The Thoroughbred hunter is not only expensive to purchase but his constitution is usually far less robust than his humbler brethren, and he is less likely to be able to rough it if turned out during the day in a New Zealand rug. In addition, it is as well to remember that the fastest horse can also be the slowest — a fact that cannot escape one's attention, if he is of the sort that requires turning three times round a large field when one wishes to pull up at a check.

For the owner-groom of limited time and means the Thoroughbred may well prove to be a luxury beyond his reach, and he is probably better off with a horse of more plebeian stock or, if he is a lightweight, with something carrying a fair amount of pony blood.

I have delightful memories of days in Leicestershire on a 14 h.h. pony who, whilst he had no hope of keeping up with his long-striding companions on the flat, was never far from the front because of his extraordinary ability to jump anything at which he was pointed.

Out of the grass countries, all but the best schooled Thoroughbred may become a positive embarrassment, whilst still demanding the ultimate in stable-care.

In the heavily wooded countries, or in the ploughs of East Anglia, for instance, the Leicestershire horse, with certain exceptions, can be an exasperating as well as a dangerous conveyance. Denied the big grass fields in which he can stretch out and jump his fences cleanly, and asked, instead, to creep and crawl and negotiate awkward places, often having to take his turn in a line of waiting horses, it is more than likely that he will show his resentment by fussing and fuming and becoming well-nigh uncontrollable.

In these conditions, the not so highly strung half- or three-quarter bred horse, the cob and the quick, balanced pony type come into their own.

In many hunts the Welsh Cob, the Fell and Dales ponies and the Highland, although the latter have an in-bred aversion to plough, make ideal mounts. They are not fast, but they are fast enough for most provincial countries, and their highly developed sense of self-preservation results in a comforting ability to get themselves out of awkward spots, whilst causing the minimum of apprehension to their riders. These larger native breeds are also up to a great deal more weight than might be supposed at first sight, and if they lack the scope to tackle the really big fences, how often is the average provincial rider asked to jump much higher than 3 feet or so?

First and second crosses with these larger native breeds, and the smaller ones, too — the Welsh, Connemara and Dartmoor and so on — produce neat, balanced hunters who besides having more scope retain much of their pony sagacity. Perhaps as important as anything is their hereditary toughness. All of them, if properly fed, thrive when turned out in New Zealand rugs and they are rarely sick, sorry or lame.

Although the Arab, the progenitor of the Thoroughbred, has had the strongest influence on almost every one of the world's breeds, the purebred is rarely seen in the hunting field. The Anglo-Arab, combining the scope and speed of the Thoroughbred, with the stamina, gaiety and courage of the Arab, is a magnificent horse and a superb hunter, but the rough and tumble in the mud and wet of an English winter does not seem to *suit* the 'horse of the desert' in his pure state.

His stamina and soundness is beyond dispute, but he has an aversion to water, quite understandable in view of his background, a particular intelligence and independence of his own and sometimes an unconventional manner of jumping. Whatever the reason, he is not usually seen indulging in the sport of the countryside — it may be, of course, that his small stature makes the fences appear larger to his rider than they really are.

It would be impossible to think of hunting and horses without including the Irish hunter. He is now very much more expensive than he once was, and some of them can be very rum customers. The best, however, are almost as much bred to the game as is the Lippizaner to the high-school work of the Spanish Riding School. They get used to crossing stone-walls and the fearsome banks of their native country before they are even broken, and they develop a knack of doing so that never leaves them.

Whatever the shape, size or capability of the horse, be he the lordly Thoroughbred or the humble cob of indeterminate birth, one thing is certain, the better schooled and balanced he is the better will he do his job in whatever circumstances he finds himself.

It is true that you can enjoy hunting without a horse, but how much more fun it is with one!

Grand National winner in 1964, Team Spirit, reappears for a day's hunting with the Old Berks. Hunt. He is here ridden by the wife of the jockey who rode him to victory.

Members of the Mid-Surrey Farmers' Drag Hounds negotiating a ditch.

The Lady Master and a huntsman of the Surrey Union Foxhounds before proceeding to a draw.

*Nicholas Selby, 18 months old, on Mokey,
a 32-in-high Shetland pony, drinks his
stirrup cup with the rest of the Quorn Hunt.*

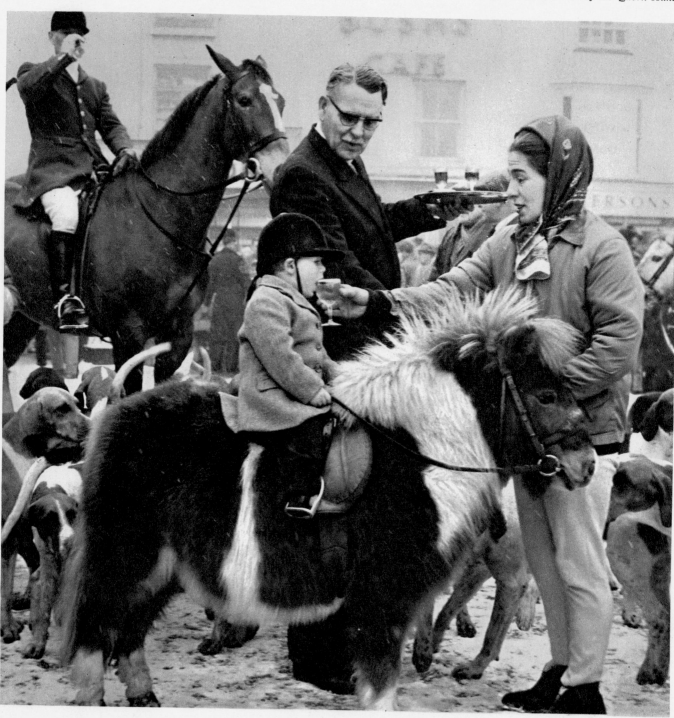

Britain's oddest hunt. The miners of Banwen
in the Swansea Valley have formed their
own hunt with hounds given from
neighbouring hunts and Welsh ponies all
belonging to the Master, Farmer Jones.

The Southdown Foxhounds leaving
Novington Manor with the first whip,
Robin Squires, in charge.

The Master of the West Norfolk Hunt with the hounds at his home Middleton Towers.

Twice a year the Norwich Staghounds meet to hunt special 'carted' deer, which are half-tamed. However, there is never a kill as the huntsmen intervene once the stag is well and truly at bay, and rescue it before the hounds can leap upon it.

The Master with the hounds in the snow at the Junior Meet of the Hampshire Hunt.

Liberty Horses performing in the circus ring.

EXIT

Many Australian stockmen have never seen a city and their excitement is hard riding over rocky ground to quell a cattle stampede or 'run', as they call it.

In true Western style a cowboy 'drives' a horse — a method of breaking it to bit and reins.

Wrestling with a steer in one of the events at the Phoenix Rodeo.

*In rodeos, where the cowboys' earnings are
calculated in seconds, the Quarter horse,
a small, heavily muscled horse, is preferred
for outrunning the steer.*

*This cowboy had only just emerged from the
pen before he was thrown.*

The Care and Management of Horses

by C. D. Ginnett, B.V.M.& S.,M.R.C.V.S.

How often do we hear that the best drivers of motor cars are those who understand how the engine works? Horrible though such a comparison may seem, the same principle applies to the relationship between ourselves and our horses or ponies. Simply to be able to stay 'in the plate', i.e. in the saddle, is not enough, and those who are content to do so with no interest in the magnificent anatomical structure of the horse, how his body functions and his management in health and disease, are unworthy of his affections, and would be well advised to acquire a bicycle. In appreciating him in all aspects of his private life we become horsemasters, as well as mere horsemen and horsewomen, with a knowledge of our friend that comes from understanding, rather than from a rigid obedience to all the 'dos', 'don'ts' and 'one must nevers' that seem to fill his world at first sight.

It is easily forgotten that our horses and ponies once roamed wild in large herds. The individual who was not blessed with the hardiness to fight long winters and illness, or with the fleetness of foot to escape his enemies, sadly, therefore, did not survive. Man noticed the strength and speed of the horse and decided to capture and tame him, because these qualities were just what he was looking for. That is where the trouble began. Today, instead of being lost in the normal process of nature, the poorer specimens can survive, and by breeding pass their defects on to their progeny and thus the species as a whole. When things go wrong we should remember that, for our own betterment or pleasure, we have created an unnatural world for the horse, so that he has become very dependent upon us for his health and happiness.

For his diet the horse relies entirely on plant material; we say he is a herbivore. Grass is his natural food and a horse of suitable size for an adult to ride will eat roughly one hundred pounds or seven stones by weight in a day, because grass is three-quarters water. This process obviously takes a long time, and since he has a small stomach which does not stretch easily, he cannot bolt it all down at once like us. By drying grass to make hay, thus removing much of the water,

man found that the horse need only eat one third as much, but none of the food value was lost and since it did not take so long to eat, instead of spending all day grazing, the horse then became available for work too. Similarly, even less corn is required than hay because as well as being drier, it is very high in 'energy ingredients' and is therefore fed according to how active the horse is required to be. Thus, from a feeding point of view, we move him from pasture into the artificial life of the stable to reduce his eating time and so increase his resting time and working capacity.

These changes in diet must be gradual. The digestion, like the muscles, must be slowly conditioned to its new function because different proportions of digestive juices are required for grass, hay and corn respectively. It is often taken for granted that a stabled horse, who will no longer be getting his 'three-quarters' of water from the grass, may require up to fifteen gallons of fresh water a day. He relies only on what we make available to him, and errors of feeding are one of the most unforgivable causes of colic. This term applies to any abdominal discomfort in the horse, which may vary from slight griping pains to unbearable agony which makes him so frantic that he is very dangerous to handle. All colics however slight, should be regarded seriously and quickly treated before they progress too far, with, perhaps, fatal consequences.

Sufficient books on feeding and stable management have been written to fill a large library, but a word about our many ponies who live outside all the year round seems in place. Like all plants, grass alters according to the season in palatability, water content and nutritional value, all of which affect the appetite. Ponies love the lush growths of spring, but, as well as blowing them out like balloons, they are more susceptible to a desperately painful condition of the feet called 'laminitis' or 'founder', the results of which can damage them permanently. Alternatively, in winter, the greater proportion of the poor, tasteless and often muddy or frozen grass must be used simply to grow a woolly coat and keep warm, so they should be given good hay to appetite, or

all but the very hardiest will 'fall off' in condition. If they are ridden regularly they may need corn feeds as well. This applies especially to youngsters and older ponies past the prime of life, which we usually consider to be from about five to eleven years old. They have their natural protections against the cold but these come from being well nourished and allowed to acclimatize slowly. If this is understood they will be quite happy; if not, then we are guilty of cruelty and should get out that old bicycle again.

A further cause of digestive troubles in grazing horses are worms. To us humans this sounds horrific, in fact, it is not really, unless there are too many of them, and anyway we must accept nature as she is, if we are to succeed in our horse management. Suffice it to say that an infected horse may, via the droppings, deposit a million microscopic eggs on the pasture in one day, each one capable, in theory, of developing into a worm if eaten by another horse. Common to many infectious diseases, young animals are more likely to become ill, and dosing to kill these parasites should be as much a matter of routine as regular shoeing.

Horses' teeth, unlike our own, are constantly growing and this is prevented from getting out of hand because they are worn down by their opposite number in the top or bottom jaw. Indeed, it is by the amount of wear that we are able to estimate his age. All is well so long as the opposite teeth match, but if, for some reason, they do not, then razor-sharp edges develop and life, and especially eating, becomes miserable for our friend. Again, regular inspection of teeth, and especially those of older horses, is imperative, so that the sharp edges can be filed or 'rasped' off, a sensation which many horses appear to enjoy.

It is often said that routine is the secret of good management, and while this may unjustly imply that the horse is a dull animal, it is sound reasoning. Since we cannot explain things to him he can only rely on instinct, trust and past experience. Anything new, startling or painful may therefore cause him to be afraid and his natural and reasonable reaction will be to fight or try to run away, according to

To a horse a broken leg once meant a death certificate. Today it can break a leg twice and recover. This Thoroughbred foal has twice broken its leg in six months, but the leg has nearly mended and the plaster cast will soon be off.

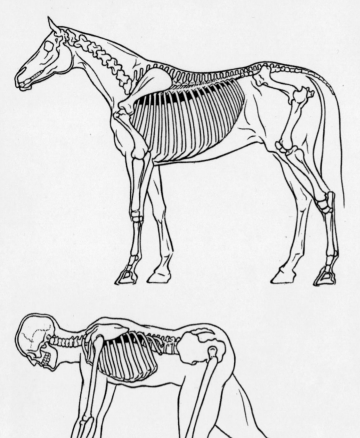

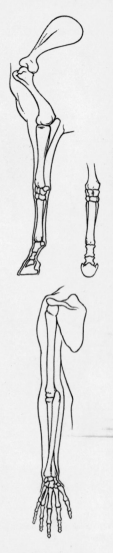

I. (Left) Much more of the weight of the body of the horse is supported by the forelegs than the hind, and, while we actually sit on the horse's spine, when we grip with our knees we help to transfer some of our weight onto the strong ribs as well.

II. (Right) In this diagram we can see that the bones in the man's arm are drawn out of proportion with those of the horse. This is quite deliberate in order to compare the human and equine limbs joint by joint; the diagrams are purely illustrative, and not accurate anatomically.

his character. With this in mind, his management should be directed towards keeping all his associations pleasant ones, because if they are not he will certainly remember the next time. The family pony that you can do anything with has developed a confidence that all will be well, because he or she has never had any reason to think otherwise. While obviously horses and ponies have widely differing characters and senses of humour too, the same basic principle applies to them all; no matter how great their intelligence, individuality and beauty, they are animals, and to expect of them, for whatever sentiments, human feeling and reasoning is wrong and unfair.

Whether they be much-loved ponies, hunters, racehorses or breeding animals our horses should be 'sound'. Ideally, this means free from any form of defect whatsoever, either bodily or functionally, so it can be argued that such a perfect animal is very rare. The controversy and technical jargon surrounding the million and one ailments which may be 'unsoundnesses' is unending, because when all is said and done we may only so often express a well-informed opinion, unlike our mechanical friends who can actually inspect the pieces. Again, man has taken the horse and robbed him of his

natural balance by sitting on top of him, placed hard metal shoes on his hooves to increase the severe jar from hard roads, and often asks him to sustain long and violent exercise, all of which place stresses and strains on weak points in his anatomy. Small wonder that a large proportion of ailments are related to the bones, joints and muscles, especially those of the legs and feet.

From his outward shape or conformation, we might imagine the skeleton of the horse to be very different from our own. In fact the basic bone structure is similar with differences in shape, length and angulation of the bones (Fig. I). For example, whereas man has developed fingers and toes for his fiddly jobs, the horse has dispensed with them, and walks on the equivalent of our middle or longest finger only in the foreleg, with the human nail adapted into the form of the protective hoof. The remains of our thumb are present in the horse as the chestnut, and our second and fourth fingers as the two splint bones, while the little finger is lost completely (Fig. II).

Man's limbs are very flexible, enabling him to move in all directions, but any engineer knows that increased movement means less strength. Thus the joints in the horse's legs function almost entirely

backwards and forwards only. In addition the limbs are fixed tightly beside the body by short, fat muscles, which are much more powerful than their long, thin counterparts in man, whose arms and legs stick out like the branches of a tree.

When muscles are required to maintain their power, but increase in length, they have strong elastic extensions attached to them. Prime examples of this are the famous back or 'flexor' tendons of the lower limbs, which transmit the actions of the muscles higher up the legs to the feet, at the same time allowing the legs to remain only the thickness of a human wrist, because at the gallop, they move very fast, and so must be light. In general terms, the hind-quarters produce the thrust and the fore-quarters and fore-limbs absorb the resulting strain and convert it into forward momentum by acting as a pivot. If we think for a moment of a steeplechaser weighing over half a ton, landing from a jump of five feet at 30 m.p.h. on two areas, each no larger than the base of a coffee pot, it is easier to appreciate the true perfection and strength of this system of levers. The fetlocks will be almost touching the ground to absorb the strain.

Horses are never said to limp; they go lame, short or uneven, favour or feel a leg,

*A decorated Shire horse at the Montgomery
Show.*

The Rothmans coach at the Easter
Van Horse Parade at Regents Park.

*The Amateur Driving Marathon at the
Richmond Royal Horse Show.*

The Watneys 'Red Rover' coach on a run from London to Brighton.

...od etc. These are but a few of the
...hs which all mean the same thing.
...will throw his head up at the walk
...rot when the painful foreleg contacts
...ground, in order to try to take the
...ght off it, so that he appears to nod
...ead when the sound leg strikes the
...nd at the next step. Detection of
...exact site or 'seat' of lameness is often
...lled task, and suffice it to say that
...urther one travels down the limb the
...likely is it to be found. One of the
...nal features of any tissue damage is
...it swells so that, within the hard hoof,
...may be tremendous pressure and it
...sy to see why foot troubles are
...fore so distressing to the horse.
...s a creature of action and any faults
...legs or feet, however slight, will
...ce his usefulness; hence John Jorrocks'
...us expression, 'no foot, no 'oss'.
...e is frequently asked why it is that
...s who break bones may often, sadly,
...to be destroyed. Incidentally,
...res are seldom caused by direct
..., but are usually due to some
...ard or abnormal movement so that
...entarily great strain is placed on
...k spot in the bone. The treatment of
...s relies on replacing the bones in
...on, and then holding them in place
...they heal, which may be a matter of
...hs. Firstly, the pull of the muscles in
...s is so strong that it is often
...sible to reposition the fragments;
...dly, the strength of the cast or splint
...red to hold them still would need to
...ossal; and thirdly, since the horse
...temporarily manage on three legs
...dog he will immediately try to use
...and thus undo all the good work,
...he is bodily suspended off the
...d in slings for a long period. Always
...sing that this is all successful, it is
...unlikely that he will ever recover
...etely normal function, and the
...ent will cause him much pain and
...tion. When we understand these
...erations it is easier to see why it is
...e and kind to put him out of his
...as quickly as possible. Exceptions
...rule may be foals, whose young
...heal readily, and those cases where
...ces don't actually separate and are,
..., only cracks.
...each breath oxygen from the air
...from the lungs into the bloodstream,
...pumped by the heart all over the
...When the horse exerts himself his
...needs more oxygen, so that as well
...ly speeding up, the heart and
...ust work efficiently. Horses cough
...ariety of reasons, infections and
...ise, so this should always be
...d seriously and advice sought,
...mismanagement can have
...ent and drastic consequences. One
...h is 'broken wind', when the lungs
...incurably damaged. Again we
...ar it said that a horse 'makes
...or is a 'whistler' or 'roarer' at fast
...nd these terms apply to a resonance
...n the larynx by the inrush of air,
...e muscles associated with the
...rds are partially or completely

paralysed. These are only examples of
respiratory troubles, but in most cases the
amount of air available to the body, and
therefore oxygen, is reduced so that the
performance suffers, which is why
faults of breathing are high on the list of
serious unsoundnesses.

At rest the heart beats about thirty to
forty times a minute, which is fifty
thousand times in every twenty-fours
hours, so that over a lifetime of activity it
is wonderful that it does not go wrong
more often. When it does it is usually due
either to faulty valves, when a 'murmur'
may be heard with the stethoscope, or else
some defect in the heart's own nervous
control causing one of the many forms of
heart block. The result is that the heart
becomes a less efficient pump, unable to
respond when the body asks it to work
harder in exercise. The effects of this are
very unpleasant for the horse and as well
as leading to loss of 'keenness', they can
alter his character completely. Heart
troubles are not common but they are
certainly serious unsoundnesses. While on
the subject of the heart and its functions,
it is worthwhile to remember that roughly
one fifteenth of a horse's weight is blood,
so that a large pony may lose at least half
a gallon without any drastic consequences.

Anyone who has bravely struggled to
read this far may well have formed the
impression that, although we have only
touched on the subjects of management
and ailments, such a thing as a happy,
healthy horse can scarcely exist! Of course,
this is quite untrue, and so long as we
know what we are doing none of these
terrible things need ever occur. To look
after our horses and ponies properly it is
not enough simply to have our good
intentions at heart; we must be able to
put them into practice as well.

*A horse on the operating table at the Animal
Health Trust's Research Station, Newmarket.*

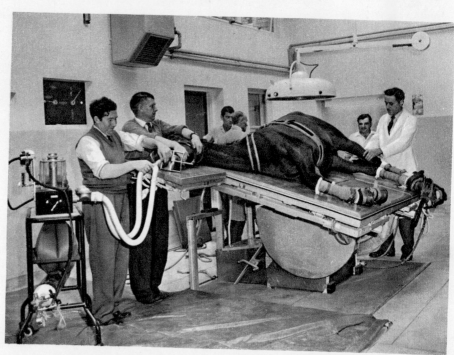

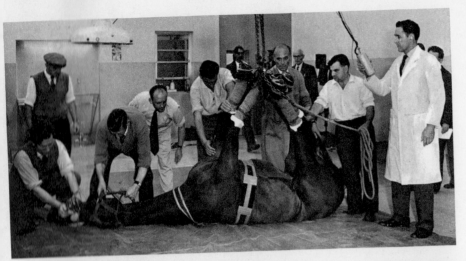

A horse being lifted by an elect
the Animal Health Trust's Equ
Station, Newmarket.

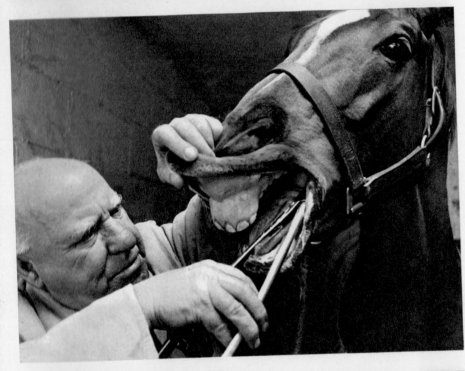

Britain's only full-time horse
extracting a tooth. In 40 yea
dentistry, Mr Humble has n
injection — he relies solely o
persuasive talking.

Morgan, a former pit pony
at the Animal Health Tru
Station at Newmarket. H
study the effects of drugs

A horse surgeon checks the condition of a horse's heart by means of a cardiograph machine.

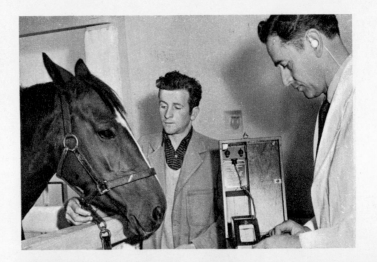

A horse ambulance. An injured horse can be moved painlessly by means of a giant sling, a mechanical hoist and a moveable floor into the ambulance and thus be carried to the operating table.

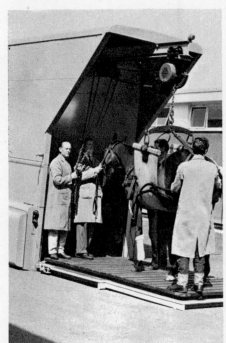

A girl horse-ranger at the Richmond Royal Horse Show feeds one of the competitors.

A pit pony in Yorkshire gets a new pair of shoes.

Five Pony Club members prepare to clean up the stables at a working rally at Ruislip Riding School.

Heroic Horses

by Stephanie Denham

Nobody questions the use of a horse. They have carried goods, pulled ploughs, provided entertainment and carried man both for pleasure and into battle, for centuries. They have a kind of inbuilt heroism which nobody questions — and yet which is occasionally taken very much for granted.

Of the millions of horses which have served man throughout history, the names of only a few live on — and mainly because they belonged to famous people. A great deal of Napoleon's success was due to the expert way in which he led his cavalry into battle. Napoleon himself always rode beautiful Arab or Barb horses, and although this was undoubtedly a great honour for a highly trained charger, it was a doubtful privilege in many ways — particularly as Napoleon is said to have lost no less than eighteen of his horses in battle!

But still their names live on . . . Kurden, Vizir, Wagram, Intendant, Coco, all carried the great man into battle, but the most famous of them all was undoubtedly the handsome white (although some say light grey) charger, Marengo. Napoleon was so impressed by his new horse's courage and speed that he named him after the brilliant French victory at Marengo. He rode his horse to several battles before his fateful day in June, 1815, when the French were defeated at the battle of Waterloo. After the battle, Marengo was brought to England where he lived the rest of his days as a true war hero in peaceful stables and fields.

While Marengo was being admired in France, another horse was achieving fame in England — Copenhagen, the famous charger which belonged to the Duke of Wellington. This beautiful horse was said to have been almost as famous as the Duke himself and many people were amazed at the horse's stamina and courage. The Duke was given Copenhagen in 1812 and he rode him to hounds, and into battle.

Copenhagen and the Duke did much to boost the morale of troops with their steadfast, daring appearance on the battlefields. But it was at Waterloo that the name of Copenhagen was made. The day before the famous battle, the Duke

and his chestnut charger rode nearly sixty miles between the various headquarters of the Prussian troops. The next morning, the Duke was again up early and he and Copenhagen set off. Together they rode through the entire battle of Waterloo, seventeen hours in all. During this time, Copenhagen behaved so fearlessly and dashingly that he was a constant inspiration to all the men — and probably an example to the tired horses too!

After many years in retirement, Copenhagen died in 1836 at the age of 28. He was buried with full military honours at the Iron Duke's country seat, Strathfield Saye, and the epitaph reads:

'God's humble instrument, though meaner clay
Should share the glory of that glorious day.'

But, although these famous men's horses will go down in historical records by name, every cavalry soldier who ever went into battle would undoubtedly have thought of his own horse as the greatest hero of them all.

Although thousands of horses went to the First World War, many never to return, the Second World War saw the end of horses in battle. Even so, they still had their part to play. In the bombed cities, police were controlling rescue work, traffic and people, as they cleared the chaos, and they were frequently mounted on horseback.

P.C. Thwaites was riding police horse Olga one day in 1944. He was controlling the traffic in London when the wailing sirens quickly cleared the busy streets for him. There was no time for a man and a horse to get under cover, and in any case, the flying bombs were already overhead. With a tremendous explosion, four houses fell like a row of matchboxes. Thwaites felt Olga tremble with fear as the flames leapt up to the sky. But worse was to follow. A plate glass window of a shop shattered right in front of them, completely covering them with debris. Olga reared, turned and bolted down the street. She just had to get away from that terrifying place.

Thwaites held on as best he could, but

this was the first time he had ridden Olga. However, he need not have worried too much because about 100 yards down the road, Olga stopped. Gently, P.C. Thwaites turned her round and led her back to the heat and chaos of the bombed area. And there, Olga, now quiet and calm, worked fearlessly and tirelessly as P.C. Thwaites controlled the arrival of rescue workers and fire engines.

Three P.D.S.A. Dickin Medals were awarded to horses during the last war. Olga was one of the proud medallists, and the other two were also presented to police horses. Upstart and his rider were also showered with broken glass and debris but the brave horse remained quietly on duty until everything had been dealt with. Police horse Regal narrowly escaped death when her stables at Muswell Hill were burnt down after direct hits by incendiary bombs. Although she was injured, and in grave danger of being burnt, she kept calm and allowed herself to be led through the smoke and flames to safety.

Fortunately, in peacetime there are fewer opportunities for horses to behave so heroically. Riots all over the world still push police horses to the lengths of their endurance, and television has given us the opportunity to marvel at the perfect training and mentality of these beautiful creatures.

From time to time, 'civilian' horses make the news. Gracie was one of Whitbread's magnificent shire horses which pull drays through the streets of the city of London each day. They are such a common sight that few people give them more than an admiring glance as they pass by. This was the case one morning in October, 1953, when Gracie and her less experienced companion horse were slowly pulling a dray through the streets of Shoreditch. Although at first glance, everything seemed to be normal, a keen-eyed observer would have noticed that the reins were lying loosely on the horses' backs, and that the driver, Charlie Gardener, was slumped forward in his seat.

Gracie had sensed that something was wrong immediately she felt the reins go slack, so she took charge of the situation. Gently leading the other horse by her side,

*When Bill Salisbury, Lucy Glitters'
groomsman, collapsed, she lay down beside
him to keep him warm until help arrived.*

*Police horses trying to hold back the rioting
crowd during an Anti-Vietnam War
demonstration outside the American
Embassy in Grosvenor Square, London.*

Olga, the police horse, showing her affection for P. C. Thwaites. Working in the midst of falling bombs, Olga had displayed tremendous courage in London during the war, and for this she won the Dickin Medal.

Charlie, the last
working survivor
of the thousands
of horses which
have been part of
the railway scene
in Britain, pulls
his own wagon for
the last time.

she did the best thing that was within her power — she pulled the dray back to her stable in Garrett Street, Clerkenwell. Outside, she neighed and stamped her hooves on the tarmac until the stablemen ran out to see what was wrong. They quickly helped poor Charlie down and got him medical attention as quickly as possible, grateful that Gracie had had the sense to come straight home. Gracie had certainly lived up to the proud tradition of Whitbread's fine shires, for they are said to descend from the very horses which rode into battle at Agincourt!

A horse can help man in so many ways. Many lives have been saved by a horse's fantastic sense of direction. A snowy wilderness in Canada can be terrifying indeed if the driver of a horse-drawn sledge should lose his way, or as so often happens, finds himself travelling around in circles. If only all lost travellers had remembered to give their horses their heads, they would have immediately headed for home. This may be a rough ride, as the horse will bump the sledge across difficult and untrodden ground in his efforts to make the right direction, but the sight of a recently trodden track and the cheering sight of home again, has filled many men with gratitude for their horse's instinct.

During the First World War, soldiers were often saved from drowning by their horses. Should the ship in which they and their horses were being transported overseas sink, they were more than grateful if they found themselves near to their horses. If a horse recognized his master's call, he would gladly swim towards him and let him clamber on to his back. The intelligent creature would then strike out and head straight for the shore.

Horses often seem to know when a man or woman they know is unhappy or unwell. Lucy Glitters arrived at Oak Tree Farm, Little Budworth, Cheshire in 1966. She soon got to know Bill Salisbury, the groomsman and odd job man, and Bill would watch her jump in the shows she entered — often rewarding her afterwards with a carrot or two. One evening in November, 1968, Bill was taking Lucy her evening meal in her stable when he collapsed by her side. The poor man was not wearing a jacket, and he could neither move nor shout for help. Lucy came over to him and lay down beside her old friend. Then she licked his hands and face, breathed on his cold body and snuggled herself against him in an effort to keep him warm. For nine long hours the two lay together — on a very cold, winter night with the stable door wide open.

Mrs. Schwabe, Lucy's owner, first noticed the stable door was open in the morning. When she went in to investigate, she was amazed to find Bill lying there. She immediately sent for the doctor, and Bill was soon tucked up in bed. And everyone had to admit that Lucy Glitters had, in all probability, saved Bill's life.

Horses have been taken for granted for centuries. Some people dismiss their past efforts to carry us into war, to pull our ploughs and carts, to carry us around and even to entertain us at the races, as being 'their duty'. Many acts of heroism are dismissed as 'instinct' and yet . . . how can we be sure?

What made Olga stop in mid charge as she ran away from the bombed areas, only to return to the very place that had frightened her out of her wits? What made Lucy Glitters stay by her old friend when she could have walked out of the stable door? These questions will probably always remain unanswered, together with thousands like them, but they do make us ask ourselves *why* we take a horse for granted when they have given us so much — including life itself!

(Below) A pit pony coming off duty after a day of dragging coal up from the mines.

(Bottom) Imp, short for Imperial, outside Buckingham Palace during his training for being ridden by the Queen in the Trooping the Colour Ceremony.

Feeding time for four of London's cart-horses.

A group of Shire horse mares on a farm in the Fens.

An autumn ploughing scene in the Westmorland Fells.

Harrowing with three horses on a farm in Westmorland.

Two Shire horses showing their paces.

A show Palomino pony.

Wild Exmoor ponies being auctioned.

A wild Palomino pony.

Wild Icelandic ponies grazing in their native land.

New Forest colts at play.

A Welsh pony and foal.

A contented pony free to roam in the wild

A newly born donkey foal.

Zither, a 2-week-old pony at Whipsnade Zoo.

Crown and Anchor owned by Whitbreads at the Easter Van Horse Parade at Regents Park.

A shepherd on
horseback, riding the
range in Patagonia.

Two Welsh
Mountain ponies
with their foals.

Various pictures of
the wild horses of
the Camargue.

*Pony-trekking in
Rhayader, Wales.*

*Setting off on a trek
across Dartmoor
in Devon.*

The winning team ride into the ring to be presented with their awards in the final of the Prince Philip Cup for the Pony Club Mounted Games Championship at Burghley.

Crossing a stream during a day's riding.

Donkeys

by John Nestle

Only a few years ago donkeys to most of us appeared in the guise of amiable or obstinate animals, reminiscent of our childhood or of rides on the beach, certainly not as a part of our adult lives. Now they are quite a proposition both as pets, companions or as a business — in fact one appeared as Donkey of the Year in the Personality Parade at the Horse of the Year Show at Wembley. And what a personality — unperturbed by music or limelight he advanced with dignity towards the Royal Box to the tune of the Donkey Serenade. His name was Ascension, his owner Mrs. V. E. Martin, his sire Forest King and his dam Bathsheba, and he had never been beaten since he won his first championship, so he could hardly fail to realize that he was indeed a V.I.P. Gone indeed are the days when few of us ever considered the breeding or pedigree of a donkey.

They have a long history, as they are one of the earliest domesticated animals and have always gone along with us from the very distant past until the present day, sometimes popular, sometimes ignored, often ill-treated, frequently revered. Their milk filled Cleopatra's, bath, their flesh is sometimes eaten, they are charming companions, undoubtedly have a sense of humour, can be extremely useful or just delightful, but always highly individual pets. With our usual human illogicality we can at the same time starve and neglect them, and yet respect them because of their religious associations. Indeed the donkey is featured in many legends and by some people he is regarded as a symbol of good luck.

Few people have ever understood the donkey as well as Robin Borwick, who, indeed, was responsible for making us realize the part they could play — and now do play — in modern life. He fell a victim to the charms of one donkey bought as a pet for his children, and almost immediately he became so involved in them that he started a stud near Maidenhead, Berkshire. To him they were almost people and every one of them knew it. He made a most extensive study of their history and from him we learn, that in the distant past the horse and pony existed in wild herds in the more fertile

pastures of the plains, and were dependent on speed as a means of self-preservation, whereas the wild donkey avoided the plain. He was of a quieter temperament, smaller, less fleet of foot, and allowed himself to be driven from the good land to the foothills and the edges of the desert, in other words to the marginal pasture. This has helped to make him far less selective in his diet than is the horse and he can thrive on less good vegetation. His loud voice could carry messages to friends on a neighbouring hillside and with his large ears he could hear their answer.

In Ancient Egypt the donkey became the friend of man a long time before the horse was domesticated and as we know from the Tenth Commandment, 'Thou shalt not covet thy neighbour's . . . ass', the Israelites made full use of the donkey. He is still much used in southern European countries and in the Middle East. On the island of Cyprus he can be seen ridden or carrying young trees upright for transplantation, and here indeed he looks well and happy. In the rocky peninsular of Gargano in Italy, parts of which are green and fertile, the donkey is far more useful than any other form of transport, as nothing else can cope with the terrain, and here also he is not only a great worker, but obviously well cared for.

In some parts of Italy his personality is greatly respected. He is most superbly harnessed and decorated, and moreover achieves a certain fame. Fortunately the donkey is fitted to work in hot climes, for his coat does not grow as closely as that of the horse.

All sorts and sizes of donkeys crop up in different countries and some of them are quite magnificent. But not all of us know that the horse and the ass (as well as the onager and the zebra) belong to the same family. It is thought that the donkey as we know him is descended from the dwarf Nubian ass, which is very small and has quite a lot of charm. He has the usual donkey markings, which include stripes in the shape of a cross on his back, the same big, soft, furry ears, outlined in a darker shade with mushroom fluff within, large intelligent eyes and pretty little side whiskers on his jowl.

In the wild state they are very small, extremely shy and live on little food of any real value. This leads us to the type of donkey whose place is in our orchard or garden or even our house, and how to look after him. Should he be the ballerina-type, of great elegance and dainty movement, or should he be more solid and homely?

At one time the solid, homely donkey who pulled a small governess cart, or was ridden by children in the country or on the sands, was more usual. But perhaps the ballerina-type is the donkey of today. He too, is sturdy, and consequently he can do the odd job very efficiently, and yet also looks extremely smart if properly turned-out with a nice little trap. But he is more elegant and more suited to modern life than his immediate predecessor, and as he traces back to the Nubian ass, there should be little difficulty in reproducing this type if we wished to do so

The modern donkey is more than just a status symbol, he is also a means of escape from complicated tensions of life. From him can be learnt a simple philosophy and he will make us laugh, as well as provide intelligent companionship at a minimum cost — unless, of course, we go in search of glory in the show ring. Even that can be done very reasonably with a donkey.

They come in all colours. They may be grey, very pale and elegant, or almost black, or various shades of brown, or completely black with no trace of brown or any other colour, other than the white underside which is so common to many of them. In Britain there are few white donkeys but there are roans. In horses one has strawberry- or blue- or grey-roan colours, in fact the word roan is used to describe a coat which is flecked with single white hairs. Real chestnut donkeys are rare and much sought after.

'Coloured' or unusual donkeys are more expensive than ordinary ones. Some are pink (a paler colour than chestnut), or apricot or treacle-coloured or rust-red. Others are 'broken-coloured' i.e. piebald (black and white) or skewbald (brown or any other colour and white) or Appaloosa (white with small black markings of thicker hair in the body coat). In addition

to this variety of shades some donkeys are also dappled. It may be quite a temptation to a donkey judge to put up an unusually coloured donkey, but this should never be done at the expense of make and shape and movement.

Here are some notes on the conformation, points and type of the donkey, prepared by the President of the Donkey Show Society, R.S. Summerhays.

HEAD. Short rather than long, muzzle very small and tapering, the flesh soft and very delicate. Profile concave (dished). The whole light and most pleasing.

JAWS. Generous, round and widely open.

EYES. Of good size, set low and wide apart.

EARS. To be well and firmly set, of good shape and size in proportion to the donkey as a whole.

NECK. Within reason, the longer the better, and to join both head and shoulder correctly. The top line and the underside to be straight, showing no sign of concavity. The whole to be firm, well-fleshed and carried without drooping.

BODY. Withers practically non-existent but if noticeable so much the better. The line of back to be practically level and reasonably short. A little concavity permitted in age, tendency to roach back a fault. The more oblique the shoulders the better. The ribs to be well sprung — the deeper the girth the better.

QUARTERS. Long, wide, flat and generously fleshed, with plenty of length between the point of hip and the point of buttock.

TAIL. Set strong and high.

LIMBS. All to be straight and true with adequate bone in proportion to type. Knees flat and wide, cannon bones short. Hocks set as low as possible, clean and correct in shape. Fore and hind legs not too close, nor too wide apart. The fore legs to show no sign of being back-of-the-knee (calf knee) nor the hind to show sickle or turned-in (cow hocks).

FEET. All to be even and of good shape, hard in appearance, clean and smooth of surface. The size must be adequate to the donkey and be true to the typical donkey hoof with no tendency to a low heel.

ACTION. To be level and true at walk and trot, smart, light and active.

SIZE. There is no limit; conformation, type and presence being the essential. For description only, the Society authorizes the use of the following terms: *Miniature* — a donkey which, when adult, measures less than 9 h.h. *Small Standard* — over 9 h.h. but under 10.2 h.h. *Large Standard* — over 10.2 h.h. but under 12 h.h. All measurements to be made without shoes.

GENERAL NOTE — The donkey being a friendly, lovable and family animal, judges will have this in mind and are advised (all things being equal) to consider favourably, and place accordingly, any donkey which has these desirable attributes.

A newsletter all to themselves is now prepared for the humble donkey, and this is crammed with helpful information and famous names. The secretary of the Donkey Show Society is Mrs. Walter Greenway, Picketts Hill Cottage, Headley, near Bordon, Hampshire, and she must be kept very busy, as donkeys are now competing everywhere, their total number of entries in the various classes running into hundreds. The big shows such as the Royal Windsor and the South of England at Ardingly in Sussex include events for them, and so do many smaller ones in all parts of the country.

Whereas a pony, as said earlier in the article, is a herd animal and consequently is unhappy and does not thrive when alone, a donkey does, providing he sees enough of his owner. There is even a story of a lady who used to leave her television on for her graceful little donkey to watch through the window, when she went out in the evening.

A donkey is splendid with children as long as they are kind to him, and for the same reason has a high entertainment value. A good companion to horses, he has a soothing effect in Thoroughbred studs, and the donkey can be a perfect 'nanny' to young foals, particularly if he has been in the same ownership long enough to make him feel he has a vested interest in them.

If you decide to have one of your own you will find that his wants are simple, inexpensive (he may well cost at the most 15 shillings a week to keep) but quite definite. A shed with an opening on one side in his field or at the end of your garden, bedded down with straw, a salt lick in a holder and clean water always available are 'musts'.

He wants good summer grass to eat, with brambles and thistles for roughage; a net full of hay (except when there is so much grass in early summer that this is unnecessary); and a little concentrated food such as Silcocks coarse mixture for cattle. If this is not obtainable ask your forage merchant to make up the following mixture: one part crushed oats, one part bran, two parts flaked maize. Feed one double handful a day. Do not feed oats alone, or pony nuts except in great moderation, as they are too rich. He can also have potato peelings and old jacket potatoes, bread, cake, vegetable scraps, rose and other garden prunings. Lawn mowings should be fed sparingly, and must be absolutely fresh and scattered on the ground, not in a pile. They ferment very quickly.

Beware of yew, wheat, and chicken food is taboo, but bran and bread are safe, any meat product, lupin and laburnam seeeds. Your donkey must not graze just anywhere (for example, lawns or roadside verges) if the grass has been recently sprayed with selective weedkiller.

Finally, to quote Robin Borwick, 'Above all, a donkey needs human love and companionship.'

Donkey of the Year — this grey stallion called Ascension, has been unbeaten since 1967.

Two very sleepy donkeys.

One of the winning donkeys at the Essex County Show.

A very long-eared donkey being shown at the Taplow Horse Show.

These donkeys like eating daisies.

Donkey racing requires a lot of concentration.

Donkeys on Blackpool beach awaiting their young riders.

Assembling at the starting line for a donkey race.

The start of the 3.30 race at the Donkey Derby at the Alexandra Park Racecourse.

Very smart headgear for a horse on Morecambe front.

Many Londoners turn out for the traditional Easter Parade in Battersea Park, including Casanova, a donkey from Battersea Park Zoo, wearing an amusing carrot creation.

This tiny donkey looks rather lost.

This donkey, belonging to Robin Borwick, enjoys travelling in the front seat of the car.

This 18-year-old donkey gazes proudly at her new-born foal.

A donkey and a Collie in deep conversation.

Jack O'Donoghue, the royal trainer, has started breeding donkeys. They are kept separate from the racehorses, but here a newly born donkey foal has stopped to pass the time of day with Gay Record, one of the Queen Mother's horses.

Trekking through the Pyrenees on a mule.

A donkey pulling a cart in Estoril, Spain.

A Victorian bath-chair being pulled by a donkey at the Sandon Donkey Show.

Miniature Shetland ponies pulling a little cart at the Easter Parade of Harness Horses and Ponies at Regents Park.

The donkey Red Start taking part in the British Driving Society's meeting.

These five donkeys suddenly appeared one day from nowhere outside a a pub in Yorkshire. They were taken to the Home of Rest for Horses in Shuttleworth and will remain there in peace.

(Right) A rather mournful-looking mule.

A very new arrival at Ruffs Orchard Donkey Stud being licked by its mother.

Two elderly donkeys have a quick word with a newcomer to the Animal League's Haven for old and unwanted animals in Kent. The other inmates consist of a number of dogs, 65 cats, 11 horses, pigeons, guinea pigs and rabbits.

Hounds of the Garth and South Berks. Hunt pause to stare at the two miniature donkeys standing in their path.

Bimbo, this appealing donkey, was found by the roadside in Italy by an English couple. They decided to adopt him, continued with their holiday and eventually brought him back to England.

A donkey and a foal grazing in a meadow.

This donkey in Co. Donegal, Eire, carries the peat home in special panniers.

(Above) Lucky was half the size of a normal donkey at birth, and with his mother is one of the many attractions at Woburn Abbey.

(Right) Mother and child.

Acknowledgments

American Quarter Horse Association 109B, 110; Associated Press 19, 20—21, 24, 31; Barnaby's Picture Library 81R, 106—107, 111, 130T, 133T, 138T, 143BL, 144TL, 144TR, 144C, 151TR; Barratt's Photo Press 65; British Museum 85; Camera Press 2, 49T, 49BR, 51B, 59, 82B, 108, 109T, 137TL, 137CR; Central Press Photos 50T, 53, 60, 61, 66—67, 70, 71, 129B, 145TR, 147TR, 147C; Fox Photos 123T; Giraudon, Paris 90T; The Hamlyn Group: Michael Holford 94; Lance Harvey 39; E.O. Hoppe 13, 14, 137B; Iceland Tourist Office 133B; Keystone Press Agency title page, 29, 81CL, 99, 100, 103T, 104, 105T, 105B, 119C, 119B, 129T, 146BL, 148CR, 148B, 151TL; Leslie Lane 22B, 25T, 28, 32T, 32B, 48, 82T, 103B; The Mansell Collection 45TL, 86—87, 91, 92—93; Douglas Mazonowicz 6; Nicholas Meyjes 130C; Ministry of Public Building and Works 41, 43, 44, 45TR; Monty 30, 74B, 80T, 146TL; John Nestle 33TL, 80B, 81TR, 101T, 101B, 132T, 134B, 138B, 143TL, 145BR, 148CL; Tierbilder Okapia 9B, 10B; T. Parker 73, 130B, 131T, 134T, 137CL, 141, 145TL, 146BR; Antonello Perissinotto 90B; Photo Researchers 8—9T, 10T, 11, 12, 46—47, 79, 83B; Pony/Light Horse 15, 143CL, 143BR, 147TL, 149; Paul Popper Ltd 125B; Press Association 126—127, 128; Sport and General Press Agency 34, 49BL, 50B, 54, 62, 64, 81BL, 83T, 119T, 120, 121T, 122, 123B, 139T, 139B, 144B, 147B; Syndication International 33B, 51T, 68TL, 68TR, 68—69B, 69T, 102, 113, 121BL, 121BR, 125T, 131B, 132B, 143TR, 145BL, 146TR, 148T, 150T, 150B, 151B; Sally Anne Thompson 74T, 137TR; United Press International 16, 22T, 23, 25B, 26—27, 33TR; Roger-Viollet, Paris 89; The Wallace Collection 40, 42, 45B

Colour transparencies have been supplied by:

Central Press Photos; The Hamlyn Group; Nicholas Meyjes; Tom Parker; Photo Researchers; Photographic Library of Australia; Pictorial Press; Dick Swayne; Syndication International.